THE SECONDARY HEAD

Peter Mortimore is Professor of Education and Deputy Director, London University, Institute of Education. He was previously Professor of Educational Research at Lancaster University, and has been a teacher, researcher, member of Her Majesty's Inspectorate, director of ILEA research and statistics and an assistant education officer (ILEA). He is the co-author of *Fifteen Thousand Hours* (1979, Open Books) and of *School Matters* (1988, Open Books).

Jo Mortimore is an educational researcher and is the co-author of *Education and Disadvantage* (1982, Heinemann Educational) and of *Involving Parents in Nursery and Infant Schools* (1981, Grant McIntyre). She has worked as a teacher, lecturer and researcher, and as an Assistant Director (UK) for Save the Children Fund.

THE SECONDARY HEAD

Roles, Responsibilities and Reflections

edited by

Peter Mortimore
and
Jo Mortimore

Paul Chapman
Publishing Ltd

Paul Chapman Publishing Ltd
144 Liverpool Road
London
N1 1LA

British Library Cataloguing in Publication Data
   The secondary head: roles, responsibilities and reflections.
   I. Mortimore, Peter   II. Mortimore, Jo
   373.1200941

ISBN 1–85396–141–8

Typeset by Inforum Typesetting, Portsmouth
Printed by St Edmundsbury Press
Bound by W. H. Ware, Clevedon, Bury St Edmunds

A B C D E F   6 5 4 3 2 1

Contents

Introduction

In recent years there have appeared a number of books and articles about headship – about, for example, how headteachers spend their time or on how to develop management strategies. But there are few books that enable headteachers to speak for themselves. The role of a head undoubtedly is demanding. It can be lonely, with few sympathetic ears available when needed. It is also busy, with little time or opportunity for reflection.

In the course of our activities in the education world over many years, however, we have been struck by the eloquence and, at times, passion with which headteachers speak of their roles and responsibilities, their rewards and their aspirations. This book, one of a pair, the other being *The Primary Head*, presents an opportunity for a small group of headteachers from the secondary maintained sector (seven in England and one in Canada) to describe and reflect on what it is like to be a head or principal in charge of a school in the last decade of the twentieth century, a time (in Britain at least) of considerable educational change.

Since we conceived the idea, the need for such an account has increased. The task of headship has never been simple or easy – as is apparent from the list of duties and responsibilities published as part of the Education Act 1987. The main responsibilities include the following:

1. Defining the aims and objectives of the school and setting these out in a school development plan.
2. Management and organization of the school and the effective use of all resources.
3. Development of a curriculum – within the context of the National Curriculum.

4. General discipline and welfare of pupils.
5. Maintaining systems of record-keeping and communicating with parents.
6. Establishing and maintaining good relationships within the school as well as with parents, governors and the LEA.
7. Monitoring and appraising the progress of the school and its staff and managing appropriate staff development.

The Education Reform Act (ERA) 1988, however, introduced the most far-reaching programme of educational legislation since the 1944 Act and, though many headteachers welcomed at least some of its provisions, arguably it placed unprecedented demands on them and their staff. In this collection, only Leggatt (in Canada) is unaffected. To the already-onerous duties listed above have been added the tasks of liaising with the governing body (of which the head is usually a member) over its new role in respect of the delegated budget, its power to appoint and discipline staff and of responding to the possibility of opting out of LEA control altogether.

The requirements for change, consequent upon ERA, have produced pressure for action but have left headteachers with very little time (or energy) for reflection. Indeed, even as contributions to this book were being written, revisions had to be made to take account of modifications introduced by the three successive Secretaries of State for Education who have held power since the bill that preceded the 1988 Act was drafted.

We anticipated that ERA would figure prominently in whatever our headteacher contributors had to say. However, in order to provide a common format (which the heads were free to work around) we specified six major sections dealing with

• the background of the headteacher and of the school;
• the headteacher's personal philosophy of education;
• organization and management of the school;
• organization and management of learning;
• relationships; and
• personal reflections on headship.

We invited contributions from eight headteachers (three women and five men) whose schools were known, or who were recommended to us. They do not represent a random sample. They do represent, however, men and women of differing ages, cultures and backgrounds, working in a range of very different secondary schools in England and Canada.

In the final chapter in this collection we seek to tease out any common threads, to highlight contrasting issues and to draw any lessons for other practising or aspiring heads or policy-makers at the level of local or central government.

We hope readers – whether from these groups or interested members of the general public – will enjoy reading the collection as much as we have enjoyed editing it. We feel privileged to be part of the process – a process that, in some cases, involved clarification by the heads of their attitudes towards careers, colleagues, pupils, governors and the education service in general.

Of course, in a collection of such personal contributions, where heads and schools are identified by name, there is bound to be a certain amount of inhibition affecting what is written. On the whole, we think these heads have been remarkably frank but we are conscious, as were they, that the repercussions of too much openness can be severe. In our view, the overall impression likely to be left in the minds of readers is positive. The contributors, in the main, are dedicated professionals, more inclined to take an optimistic, rather than a pessimistic, view of the future.

Arguably, there has been no previous period of State education when teachers or headteachers have received so much (frequently negative) attention, yet have had such demands made upon them. Here eight of those at the front line present their reflections on headship. That these people are so obviously concerned about the difficulties facing headteachers and schools is a serious warning to all of us involved in the system but, especially, to those with political responsibilities for the service. These are responsible heads talking: as editors, we hope that those responsible for the formulation of educational policy will be listening.

Peter Mortimore,
Jo Mortimore,
London, June 1991

Acknowledgements

In commissioning these chapters, we were conscious that our editorial demands were daunting: requesting eight secondary headteachers (committed to the leadership of their schools at a time of great change) to pause for reflection. We wish to thank all of them for responding so splendidly to this challenge.

1
Roger Alston
William Howard School

Roger Alston began his teaching career in outer London as an English teacher in a grammar school, and later as head of department. Subsequently he became head of an arts faculty in a comprehensive school. In 1973 he moved to the Resources for Learning Development Unit in Bristol as Deputy Director. This unit was established to explore 'resource based' or 'independent' learning in Avon secondary schools. In 1980 he was appointed as deputy head at Nailsea School, Avon, and in January 1985 took up the headship of the William Howard School in Brampton, Cumbria.

THE SCHOOL

The William Howard School is a six-form-entry, mixed comprehensive school with 120 in the sixth form. It is on two sites, the upper school (years 9–13) having been built in 1950 in the red-brick 'bus-garage' mode, and the lower school (years 7–8) being a collection of modern and older buildings, the oldest (the original Brampton one-form-entry grammar school) dating back to the late 1700s. The school was formed in 1980 when the grammar school and the secondary modern were merged.

Brampton is a small market town serving a rural area. Some pupils travel large distances through beautiful countryside south of Hadrian's Wall to attend. There are pupils from isolated rural communities and small farms but, as the more affluent middle classes move into villages east of Carlisle, there are increasing numbers whose parents have high academic aspirations for them. Thus the school has a full mix of ability, background and socioeconomic status, but it is firmly mono-ethnic. The stable family life of most pupils is a significant characteristic.

PERSONAL PHILOSOPHY OF EDUCATION

I think deep down that I don't believe in schools at all. The problem is that institutions tend to deal with everyone in the same way because they have to have procedures and routines to survive. This leads them to be inflexible. But people don't all learn in the same way. Some people read the instructions, others get on with the job and learn by doing. You can't learn to ride a bicycle or drive a car by reading about it.

I believe in pupils taking responsibility for their own learning and behaviour. Schools are the last place to put children if you think this: because of sheer numbers they can only work on rules everyone has to keep, and a curriculum that has the same content and roughly the same pace for all. When pupils look back over their lives in school their memories are of trips, visits and residentials; of taking part in concerts, plays and other group activities; and rarely of their daily lives in classrooms.

In the late 1960s and early 1970s I was involved in attempts to change the dullness of institutional life, to look at pupils as individuals, and to increase the range and scope of school life. They were exciting times, when education was comparatively well resourced, but our efforts seemed, looking back, to fail. I think they failed because we were working on instinct not evidence, and because in looking for exciting new ideas we didn't challenge what we did.

If we have to have schools, and the present organization of society suggests they're here to stay, we need to *manage* this huge body of people to make it cater for the individual, make it responsive, make its environment stimulating and make it improve and develop in response to creative thinking.

ORGANIZATION AND MANAGEMENT OF THE SCHOOL

The Head's Contribution

'When the best leader's task is done the people say, "we did it ourselves" ' (Lao Tsu). Robert Townsend used this quotation in his amusing yet pertinent book on management, *Up the Organisation* (Townsend made a multinational enterprise out of a small car-hire company, Avis). No apologies here for the parallel with the business world: we still have a lot to learn about management. The quotation has a great deal to say about delegation and about how people thrive on responsibility, but it doesn't mean the manager has any less to do. The philosophy indicates a style or 'ethos'. The process of change and improvement across the whole school still needs to be co-ordinated.

No matter how we may resist the notion, the fact is that very few people react naturally to their leaders. Some may be deliberately destructive, or make 'them and us' assumptions about managers. Many want to be appreciated (and rewarded) and want to please. Whatever the case, the head sets the style and the tone. What he or she spends time on becomes important. The people who work in the school, teaching and non-teaching, are the most important and expensive resource. I think we should spend most time on them.

I have always resented those who protect themselves by red lights or secretaries with appointment books. I know full well how busy head-teachers are, but the signals that go out from this are ones of importance and status. In the Civil Service I believe status depended on the size of your carpet or your desk. I have worked in schools where status was judged on the number of keys you had or whether you had a personal telephone. One thing is certain, when people are preoccupied with status they expend their energy on increasing that rather than on improving their teaching.

Heads need to be aware that their approach gives key signals about priorities. A current danger is a preoccupation with financial affairs, fund-raising and marketing. Local management has given welcome freedom and flexibility, but any marketing person will tell you that unless the product is good the hardest sell in the world won't work.

I am aware that there are many general statements here. I hope that, in subsequent sections of this chapter, you will find concrete examples of what I mean.

Whole-School Management

We have learned much recently from the industrial and commercial worlds about management. We need to be systematic and clear about where we want to be and how we propose to get us there. I meet people in education who avoid the issue by hiding behind the difficulty of definition – people/children are not products, they are complex, and the process of educating them is as well. This complexity means we have to adopt an intuitive approach. The reluctance to analyse how learning takes place and how we can effectively manage a school or a classroom leads, I think, to loose arrangements for progress and improvement, a lack of logic and no scope for monitoring and evaluation.

The new language for management is also causing problems. People talk about 'jargon' and can become suspicious and defensive. 'Mission statements', 'targets', 'performance indicators' and 'audits' fall into this category. I feel we should not back away from these: we are beginning to use new management techniques and because they are new they need new descriptions. The old words perpetuate old thinking. Obviously we need to preserve all that has been good, but to build on this we need a new and more analytical approach. We need to ask, 'What do we want students to achieve?' and, 'What evidence will tell us they can achieve it?' This applies to the work of the whole school, and a whole-school approach to policy and priorities, providing a common framework, is the only one likely to produce consistency of change and improvement, and the sustaining of it. You can see this particularly clearly in development areas, such as information technology or equal opportunities. A student's experience must be coherent, progression has to be built in – yet the responsibility for delivery rests with different subject departments. The solution is a management one: the provision of a direction, a framework and policies that are shared, integrated and coherent.

Whole-school management at William Howard begins with the whole day of 'dedicated time', which the management team of head, three deputies and three senior teachers takes early in the autumn term, working with an outside facilitator on review and planning. When this process started we began by brainstorming the current situation – strengths, weaknesses, buildings, people, pupils, catchment, areas for development, outside perceptions, myths and legends – everything and anything we could think of. We put all this material into headings for development, remedial attention, continuation or for just ignoring. We began to prioritize and to set ourselves targets. Targets were linked to people on the management team, who were given clear statements of outcome and timescale. We considered our strengths and weaknesses both as a team and individually.

We arrived at the point where we needed a clear statement of intention, a 'mission statement' that could be shared by everyone and against which we could judge whether our goals were valid:

Every pupil will have equality of opportunity to develop their maximum potential through

- a broad curriculum
- a variety of experience

- co-operation and partnership
- academic and personal achievement
- a desire to learn.

Our school will therefore aim to provide

- an educational experience of the highest quality
- an appropriate and high-quality environment
- excellent and suitable resources to support learning and it will be
- responsive to the needs of all those involved with the school.

This is common sense, of course, and not something anyone could take exception to. Nevertheless we find it a useful point of reference. Armed with this and our targets for the next year we began the process of consultation and sharing. We are still learning about this, and getting things wrong. The usual tensions exist between a small group (the management team) that thinks it knows what it wants and how to get there, and the larger staff group. Nevertheless, we have become convinced that this process provides a way of gaining direction and control. Our next plans are to work in similar ways with different groups of staff – departments, teams implementing cross-curricular themes, teams of tutors. We know that our visions need to be shared ones, and that we need to be responsive to good ideas. This is where we must work next.

The school had five main targets in its development plan for the year in which this chapter was written:

1. *To work with departments to produce developments plans for each* This will involve our director of staffing (see below) working with these groups to establish their priorities within the overall school framework. We hope to see policies and targets related to differentiation, cross-curricular themes, equality of opportunity and more flexible teaching and learning styles. The important thing is to work towards sharing and ownership of the policies, and that the targets should be

- specific
- measurable
- achievable
- relevant
- timed.

2. *To continue to develop our processes of monitoring and reviewing the things we undertake (quality assurance)* Our head of learning support will work with departments throughout the year to help them find evidence to tell them whether or not the policies and targets in the development plans

are actually working inside classrooms. The kinds of tools we have used in the past are classroom observation, pupil diaries, interviews with pupils and teachers. The head of learning support will do some of the work herself and involve teachers in the department as much as possible. Perhaps a few words about the technique of using pupil diaries to collect evidence might be appropriate. We brief a group of pupils who will be working on a particular course, or even across different curriculum areas, about what we are looking for and ask them to record their experiences: for example, how often do you use a computer during a week and what kinds of things do you do on it? Or how many worksheets do you use in science in a month and how many times do you need to ask the teacher to explain parts of the worksheet to you? Pupils record as they go through the period of time allotted and we examine the evidence afterwards.

3. *To develop and review our in-service education and training (INSET) policy*   The school staff-development plan arises from the departmental plans. Sometimes teachers need time away from classrooms to plan and review. However, we want to bring 'experts' into classrooms to support and train teachers rather than bringing the teacher out. This will be a change of emphasis for us away from courses and meetings to trying to provide expertise to help 'on the job'.

4. *To run pilot schemes on 'action planning' (personal tutoring for students) and to review these*   We have become more and more concerned that someone should review, with students, progress over the whole curriculum. The more we adopt a cross-curricular approach to such issues as health education, information technology and environmental education the more difficult it is to ensure coherence and progression for an individual. Extra opportunities, problems of motivation and behaviour, career aspirations – all these need to be discussed with individuals, and strategies need to be agreed and reviewed. To identify the issues and to examine the opportunities and problems, we decided on the pilot schemes together with a monitoring process similar to the one in (2) above.

5. *To conduct market research in our community about the role of the school*   I will return to this later in the section entitled 'Relationships'.

Staff Management

We have become more and more convinced that time and effort working with people is our main priority. They are far and away our most expensive resource. We became convinced that we needed more skills in managing human resources than we had; as teachers we had usually gained our status not by managing but by teaching well. When one of our deputy heads took a two-year secondment to the LEA we took the opportunity to appoint a director of staffing. The person appointed (not a teacher, as it happens, but someone with a background in personnel and education) has the brief of working as a facilitator with groups and individuals, helping them – within the overall priorities and directions of the school – to set targets for themselves. It has been relatively easy to draw up priorities at management-team level but much more difficult to involve all members of staff and to achieve real sharing and ownership of priorities among the whole staff. We suspect that, though efforts are made to consult on draft documents and plans, we still suffer from the 'top-down' approach. Our director of staffing's main job is to tackle this. She has adopted a systematic, highly organized approach (similar to departmental planning, outlined above).

We have never had (or never organized properly) information about our teachers. Our director of staffing is currently establishing a personnel re-cord for each member of staff (teaching and non-teaching). It will include personal details along with qualifications, interests and scope for develop-mental plans. This will provide a background against which applications for INSET can be considered and a resource base from which tutor/mentors for internal INSET can be drawn. It also provides the basis for the staff review system, linked to job descriptions and targets and a guaranteed review. In addition, our new staffing director has identified the need for a 'shadow' staffing structure. This takes into account current staffing allo-cations, the school development plan, departmental priorities therein, and resources and national priorities. It begins with a detailed analysis of pres-ent staffing arrangements, including the allocation of allowances and pupil–teacher contact time. The shadow structure also provides a baseline for recruitment practice. A post that falls vacant is not automatically replaced with an identical one.

Teachers' morale is, currently, generally quite low – we have the dual problems of low pay and low public esteem. People need responsibilities and to feel they are succeeding and improving. The style of organization (dealt with above) helps this, but unless whole-school priorities are shared they will get no further than the pieces of paper on which they're written. Full staff meetings are not the answer, as contributions tend to come from a vociferous minority, and discussion tends to disintegrate into calls for more 'discipline' or a new coffee machine in the staff-room. Departmental meet-ings are useful for concentrating on specific task areas but not for whole-school policies. We have tried staff meetings that were broken up into small group seminars, and open working parties. Also, I don't feel a pyra-mid structure with debate at hierarchical levels is productive. All professionals should have the opportunity to take part in the policy-making process (though not all will want to), and all should have the chance to initiate policy. Our equal-opportunities policy began this way.

A management team with whole-school responsibilities needs to work creatively and in an integrated way. There will be major areas of overlap so no pastoral/curriculum demarcation lines are possible – this is bound to send the wrong signals and to create divisions within the institution. The main areas of responsibility within our management team are

- staff management and development;
- external relations;
- guidance (tutoring, action planning, personal and social issues); and
- learning support (teaching and learning styles, quality control).

Heads of department are the traditional middle-management structure in secondary schools. Departments are close-knit mini-organizations that can be remarkably effective in enabling the individuals within them to work closely together. They can also be isolationist, defensive and complacent. They are not particularly effective in dealing with 'whole-school' issues because they tend to see the educational process in 'subject' terms. Many new pressures are forcing us to look at different management models – not to replace departments (at this stage) but to run alongside them and to involve members of different departments in a dialogue with each other. Recently we appointed co-ordinators for various initiatives: equal opportunities, information technology, health education and flexible learning. The task these people have is to work through a whole-school policy, with departments making sure there is coherence and progression for individual students across the whole of their curriculum.

To do this they first have to identify what we want to see happening. Criteria and indicators have to be negotiated, agreed and shared. Legislation or 'guidelines' currently dictate content and skills. The second phase is to define what is happening now. This involves some sort of curriculum audit with an assessment of staff attitudes and training needs. We have used very rough research tools in this second phase: attitude questionnaires, pupil diaries and classroom observation aimed at revealing particular factors. We don't pretend that these processes have validity in research terms, but they do give us 'snapshots' of current practice.

The other traditional middle-management structure is the pastoral system of year heads or heads of house. Very often these roles have been seen as 'fire-fighting' ones – managing behavioural problems (a very time-consuming process) on a day-to-day basis. The whole-school approach demands a different role and a different style as the managers of teams of tutors who are involved in tutoring, counselling and 'action planning' with individual students. Time must be created so that the whole of a student's school experience is planned and reviewed on a regular basis: strengths and weaknesses, subject choices, career choices and opportunities that exist within the school and outside it. The biggest challenge for these managers at the present is to change the priorities in a system that emphasizes the value of subject teaching above pupils' learning. This is a difficult area. We are not in a position to move to a better tutorial system throughout the school, perhaps because as yet not all our colleagues are convinced that the role is an important one.

Ensuring quality has probably been the aspect of management we have spent most time on recently. From our first attempts at analysis of our current situation and how we needed to change, we were discussing effectiveness and how we would recognize it and sustain it. We began by asking the following questions:

- Is the curriculum being delivered at an appropriate level for individual pupils?
- Are there effective grouping policies?
- Is there a clear and agreed policy about the function of monitoring, recording and assessment procedures?
- Are monitoring, recording and assessment incorporated systematically into teaching and learning strategies?
- Do we have planned development targets for upgrading our environment?
- Does the school measure how effectively and efficiently staff are utilized?

We took each of the targets we had set ourselves and asked a series of questions such as these about it.

The next stage was to decide what we would need to see that would answer the question in the affirmative – the indicators. These might be written plans, policies, agreements made, lists of criteria or they might be pieces of classroom practice. Where this is the case there is an implication that someone will be observing inside classrooms in a monitoring role. As we explored the target areas more thoroughly we began to ask more and more detailed questions. We found the evidence needed to answer the questions about effective learning and assessment could only be found in the classroom.

This could be threatening, particularly if the whole process was imposed from above. We decided that the questions and the indicators needed to be discussed and negotiated fully in advance, that criteria for observation needed to be shared and that the style of the exercise needed always to be supportive and productive. I hope we are moving towards more open classrooms where having two teachers in the room, with one collecting evidence both can benefit from, is normal and acceptable or even welcomed. When our equal-opportunities working party decided that having policies and procedures was not enough, the members agreed on a mutual observation programme with specific criteria about the use of teacher time and pupil responses in terms of gender. The evidence that came from this was startling and probably had a greater effect on teaching practice than any of our previous statements or resources polices. Currently we are finding that this process of ensuring quality through carefully constructed criteria (shared by everyone involved) and a rigorous evaluation process has caused major changes in thinking.

For as long as I have worked in education and been involved with secondary schools I have seen creativity stifled by administrative tasks. As a head of department I had the stock cupboard and the order book; as a deputy head (probably the worst job of all) the 'cover', the timetable and the examinations. The ratio of teachers to non-teachers in most secondary schools is incorrect: teachers are doing administrative tasks they have neither the time nor the skill to do well. We are misusing an expensive resource.

Our forward planning involves 'converting' one deputy-head post into a main scale teacher and administrative officer. The cost is almost the same. We think that both the teaching and the administration will benefit, releasing the other deputy heads to be genuinely creative. The status of non-teaching staff needs to be high. There's no room for meetings from which they are excluded and common rooms only for teachers.

THE ORGANIZATION OF LEARNING

I welcome the concept of a National Curriculum. I won't rehearse its advantages, except to say that the major one has been to concentrate teachers' minds on the teaching and learning process instead of on which skills and content to teach. Just now many teachers are fully stretched looking at attainment targets and programmes of study to see what adjustments need to be made in concepts, skills and content. There is also the curriculum-structure debate, particularly in key stage 4, where the goal posts seem to be continually changing and the only safe course appears to be to preserve as much flexibility as possible to allow for as yet imprecise future directions.

But these are not the most interesting issues. The key challenges are the ones that were there before the National Curriculum but that have now been highlighted: cross-curricular issues, differentiation and the design and negotiation (with a tutor) of a curriculum for an individual student.

We have known for years that a charismatic teacher can work very effectively with a group of youngsters of similar ability, using a heavily teacher-led approach. But when this is the only style, or when the groups are more mixed in ability or motivation, there are problems.

The search for more flexible learning styles isn't new. My present school was involved in the 'Dalton Plan' in the 1920s. We have had programmed learning, resource-based learning and supported self-study. The problem with these has usually been enthusiasts concentrating on a particular style at the expense of all others, including class teaching. New technology, better and more stimulating resources and an understanding of both the skills teachers need to fulfil a tutorial role and how time can be found in a busy classroom to act in this role, are making new teaching and learning styles possible. Tutoring (or coaching) can be with individuals, pairs or small groups. Class lessons or discussions and group work are all used in the circumstances when they are most appropriate. As we go in for more monitoring of the learning process in the classroom, it becomes more apparent not only that this is an effective style but that it is also essential if individuals are to maximize their potential.

Words can sound vague and general: as I looked into a lower-school classroom recently I saw pupils in three groups. One group was studying slides of human bones – skulls, arms, legs. The question being asked was, how had these people died? You could see the jagged breaks and holes, and the pupils were comparing them to drawings of Roman weapons. They were working as a group with a great deal of discussion. A second group was working privately, writing up the results of research on Hadrian's Wall. Two were word-processing their accounts using computers. The third group was with the teacher, involved in a group tutorial – reviewing and planning their work. This pattern doesn't happen by accident but with careful planning, resource organization and the use of teacher time.

Two years ago when we began to address how to cope with the problems of differentiation we felt the introduction of the National Curriculum (especially assessment on ten levels) would highlight, we discussed seriously new grouping systems based on achievement rather than age. Though there are many reservations about this strategy, from discussion has come a new approach to grouping. In the past we 'locked' students into groups, in sets or of mixed ability, for at least a whole year. Now we are beginning to group more flexibly, for specific purposes at specific times.

This means as much block timetabling as possible, and teams of teachers working closely together. Grouping can then be by interest, maturity, ability or by any other criterion, and this can change during the year and at various times. This also implies a modular approach to the curriculum.

Most teachers would concede that the wide range of ability within comprehensive schools makes maximizing the potential of the most-able pupils difficult to achieve. Competition with the private sector, and open enrolment, are real pressures forcing us to make sure we achieve what we have always said we want to achieve. There are four ways of ensuring we cater fully for the most able:

1. An effective differentiation programme in classrooms, such as the one described above.
2. Very precise ability grouping.
3. Enrichment.
4. Acceleration (moving a pupil into more advanced programmes of study with older pupils).

We have chosen a mix of the first three. The enrichment programme involves either taking some pupils off the timetable for a short period (possibly a week) or abandoning the timetable for a whole year group (which is only possible later in the summer term after public examinations). Small groups of our year-8 pupils have worked with outside experts on specific projects: archaeologists on Hadrian's Wall, North West water on analysis of water purity, a classics specialist for an intensive week of Latin, a firm of architects on housing design and the editor of the local newspaper. The level of achievement in these intensive experiences is amazing and seems to justify the time missed from the normal teaching programme. Some lessons may be learnt from this. There are problems, of course, in identifying pupils for what is a different and attractive opportunity. Looking ahead, we see the need for whole programmes of these opportunities to be built into the school curriculum, with the personal tutor, who looks at the whole curriculum, negotiating and planning with the student how experiences such as this, and residentials, work experience and extra-curricular possibilities can be built into a coherent programme for the individual.

The teacher's personal tutorial role is vital and should now be a major focus for development. Teachers need new and different skills, time must be created and priorities need adjusting. I think the concept is more likely to be attractive if comparisons are made with the academic-tutor model in universities rather than if it is linked to objectives in personal and social education. There are too many personal- and social-education courses in which the goals are not clearly enough defined and in which pupils who have good social skills are treated in the same way as those who haven't – often in the name of equality of opportunity.

All of the developments we are working towards demand one important shift of attitude on the part of both teachers and learners. This is the move away from the need for constant supervision of pupils and the teacher as the only provider of information and guidance, towards more pupil responsibility for learning.

It has been generally accepted that pupils should not be withdrawn from areas of the curriculum on a regular basis for special language and numeracy teaching. With more individual programmes, pupils with special needs should have classroom support. We use our learning support staffing to put two teachers in as many classrooms as possible, particularly in years 7 and 8, and to provide a consultancy on resources and activities in other areas. Using staffing like this is much more flexible than, say, 'withdrawal' groups, for it provides for all special needs not just those that have been predefined. It allows for special consideration of pupils with behavioural problems, or the very able, as well as those with specific learning difficulties.

RELATIONSHIPS

I once tried standing at the front entrance of the school in the morning to greet everyone with a smile as they came in – both pupils and teachers. I hadn't been in post very long. A deputy head had a word with me: 'The staff find it threatening that you're checking their timekeeping already . . .'.

We are assigned roles and it can be very difficult to break the mould. The traditional authoritarian stance, however, has limited value when we change teaching styles from teacher as provider of ideas and information to co-operative, pupil-centred approaches. In fact, one works against the other. You can tell when you enter any school what kind of relationships exist between colleagues and between teachers and pupils by the way they talk to each other and the atmosphere in corridors. It's heartening to see constant interchanges and greetings as people go about their business.

We appoint people who like young people, and who are going to listen to them. We try also to send signals to the pupils that they are important. We diverted scarce resources to providing them with common rooms, with carpets, curtains, pictures, plants and pool tables. In common with many schools we have a school council, but we make sure that it can take decisions that affect directly what happens in school. 'Student services' is one of our budget headings, controlled by the council, which pupils have used to improve their own environment and the social life of the school. I refuse to be a policeman, patrolling corridors to prevent insurrection at break and lunchtimes. If we are to have co-operative working and healthy relation- ships and are to treat people as equals, the head has to be part of this. The office door has to be open to young people as well as to adults and, despite the distractions, it's good when they feel they can call in.

ERA and the new role for LEAs after local management of schools (LMS) have radically changed relationships between schools and the wider educational, industrial, commercial and parental groups. In the past we prided ourselves on a close partnership with the LEA and, to a greater or lesser extent, ignored everyone else. Whatever we would like we have to adapt to the new world where not only has everyone an opinion on how a school should be run and how to teach but also groups from outside the recognized educational world have new power and influence. How shall we respond?

Governors

A recent article in *The Independent* stated that 'Heads have no difficulty in maintaining the upper hand surrounded as they are by governors who may be well intentioned but are probably unfamiliar with the day-to-day prob- lems involved in running a school or the latest trends in educational de- velopment'. The author had missed the point about the role of governors after ERA. I think they are conscious of new responsibilities and unlikely to 'rubber stamp' the head's decisions. I know to my cost that my governing body will not. We formed sub-committees in the months before LMS but these foundered because discussions tended to be in isolation on particular areas like 'curriculum' or 'environment'. Governors have management re- sponsibility and are not concerned with day-to-day problems. Of course they need to know their school, and there are many well-rehearsed strat- egies they can adopt to achieve this, but they do not need the operational detail a head has to have. They do, however, need to be involved in the 'strengths-and-weaknesses' debate, in helping to devise the school develop- ment plan – in setting priorities – and they will want to devise their own indicators of success. This will take time and can't be achieved at a business meeting between 7.30 and 10.00 p.m.

Our governors took two whole days, together with the school manage- ment team, using an outside facilitator to consider the school development plan. The processes we used were more or less the ones that had been used previously with the management team. We asked the following questions:

- Where are we now? (What are all our perceptions of the current situation – personnel, environment, people, financial resources, pupils?)
- Where do we want to be? (The ideal – a philosophy of education?)
- How shall we get there? (Priorities and targets?)

This will not happen every year, probably once every four years, the life of the governing body, will be sufficient. What it did achieve was a real understanding of the issues and a new trust between the management team and the governors.

We followed this by establishing task groups based on the specific targets we decided upon. We now hold governors seminars once each term when all the 'target groups' report to the whole group. These meetings are miles away from the formal business meetings that were our only forum two years ago. They are creative, open and participative; a genuine dialogue takes place where no one holds an 'established' position.

One early anxiety for the 'professionals' was that governors would have different priorities and that the school would be led down paths which our teachers would not feel comfortable to follow. The reality was that we all wanted the same things.

Parents and the Wider Community

In our mission statement it says that we will be 'responsive'. This needs a conscious effort to make our large organization, and the building it sits in, welcoming to outsiders. Signposts, reception areas, telephones that are answered (have you tried telephoning *your* school recently?) people who stop and greet strangers instead of walking past – these all need a conscious effort.

In these days of open enrolment it is even more important that parents bring concerns to school rather than telling their neighbours. They will do this if they feel welcome and if they feel that something will happen if they do. Defensive reactions are counterproductive. We have set procedures that ensure that all concerns that are expressed end with an open dialogue between those concerned. We make sure parents know whom to contact, and that they have met that person face to face before. Above all we share criticism, in the hope that 'your critic is your best friend'.

Our local community uses our school every evening and at weekends, and also, crucially, during the day. Though we are well aware that our main task is to educate young people, we know that many do not stop wanting to learn at 16 or 18 years old. Local groups hold exhibitions in our school foyer (despite the enormous numbers of children and adults who use this area in the course of a day – it's not a 'protected' area – there has been only one breakage in five years). The strength of all this for the school is that people in our community feel comfortable there. The last thing we would want to do is to attempt to separate adults and children.

Links with Other Cultures

Our part of Cumbria is a long way from anywhere else. Most of our pupils live in small villages. In many ways we are cut off in the far north of England from the issues that confront those in the south or in large conurbations. There are many advantages for us: stable families, relatively low unemployment, no traffic jams – but there are disadvantages too. One worry has been that our youngsters' horizons can be low: they focus on our local area without seeing beyond it.

One of our teachers (energetic, committed and brave) met the chairman of governors of a school in Tanzania and invited him to our school. We began a link with Uru School near Kilimanjaro that, at first, involved the writing of letters and sending books and equipment. Two years ago a party from William Howard went to Uru. Twelve months ago a group of young Tanzanians came to Brampton. It's difficult to describe the effect this had not just on the school but also on the whole community. Difficult adolescent boys whom I know dislike, on principle, people from the next small town, respected the way the Tanzanians played football, and actually found they liked them. These African girls and boys were first objects of fascination and then of extreme interest. We held an assembly just before they returned, at which the Tanzanians sang African songs and danced: they had their audience completely under their spell.

We are convinced that this link must become an integral part of life in our school. No amount of emphasis in personal and social education on multicultural issues could have had half the impact this real, human situation had. Like everything else we value, this link will need to be carefully managed to ensure that it grows and develops. The co-ordination will be planned, and the team organizing the link will be changed every two years. The aims are clearly defined:

- To break down prejudice with regard to colour and life-style.
- To promote understanding between young people of both nationalities who are the future leaders of our two countries, and hence achieve better understanding between our two nations.

- To promote long-term liaison between the two schools and communities.
- To broaden experience of developing world issues, the physical environment and culture and values.
- To pool resources to improve education in both schools.

The LEA

LEAs have had their day. One year into LMS many secondary heads whom I know are clamouring for as much delegation from the centre as possible, including, now, the 'advice' part of the inspector/advisory service, transport, special needs and even the county treasurer's functions. This is because they have discovered the benefits of local flexibility in the use of resources. 'Advice' is available in other schools, from university and polytechnic departments, and many other agencies – it seems foolish to expect a few LEA advisers to be experts in everything. We have not found that the administrative burden is too great; I think the opposite is the case – a 'cheque-book' approach would positively save time spent chasing LEA departments.

However, I don't think isolationism is a good thing. There are links to be made and partnerships to be formed in this new world. Secondary schools in our area have already pooled resources to deliver a much wider range in the 16–19 curriculum, including the new 'entitlement', the Certificate of Pre-Vocational Education and Business and Technician Education Council (BTEC). The initiative has come from the schools. The new control over budgets means that the group can either pay for individual pupils to study elsewhere or can make its own appointments to deal with specific curriculum areas. All this is possible because of the new flexibility – the more co-operation under LMS rather than less.

Another link is between our secondary school and primary schools in our area. This is a natural educational community with common interests and common clients. We want to offer administrative services to the small schools in our area (some are two- or three-teacher primaries, and there are seventeen altogether). We want to share facilities and expertise, particularly in such specialist areas as physical education and music, and we want to learn from our local primary schools about their formative assessment techniques and recording procedures. It seems to me that far from facilitating links, the existence of the LEA has inhibited them. The concept of partnership is best addressed by those who can see tangible gains from it, and control over resources makes that possible.

Marketing

Various exhortations have been made to schools to generate income for themselves. Recently we examined our own opportunities in this direction and reached the conclusion that our scope was limited. Community use of our premises is unlikely to make a great deal of money. Attempts to maximize income through price rises would send out the wrong signals to our community and probably militate against the goodwill and wide community use we now enjoy. We aren't *seen* as a business. To generate large profits out of our facilities would be wrong for us.

We are by far the largest employer in our local area. Though we can find work-experience placements in small companies, major sponsorship is out of the question. We have developed good links with local industry and commerce but I wouldn't expect these small businesses to hand over large amounts of cash, and they wouldn't expect me to ask.

The answer for us is to be a popular school that attracts pupils and thus operates cost effectively. When open enrolment came along we made sure our prospectus was well presented and professional. We made a video of work in the school and distributed it to all our 'feeder' schools. We opened our doors to all prospective parents, during the school day in November and December, so that parents could see for themselves what was happening in our classrooms.

Now we propose to go a stage further. One of our targets is to conduct a serious piece of market research, aimed at all the people who live in our area whether they have children at the school or not. For the first time we aim to collect some real evidence of attitudes, needs and perceptions. I am excited at the prospect of having this evidence, and of the responses we might make.

PERSONAL REFLECTIONS

I enjoy this job more than any of the others I have had. Five years out of schools convinced me that I wanted to be back to enjoy the teamwork, the sense of getting things done, the community feeling. Inside a school is where the real power to change things lies, because so much depends on the quality of relationships, and from the outside it is difficult to build strong ones. Of course, with our new power, it's now even better. Despite the pressures, which are real, the new freedom to move resources to areas of need or development is exhilarating. However, working with people is still what I enjoy most. Teaching is a delight, though it produces tensions about use of time. I still indulge myself, possibly selfishly, because the greatest rewards of all still lie in a good lesson.

There are, though, some things that should change. The career structure for heads is not satisfactory. I think it was Oscar Wilde who said that after seven years we begin to destroy what we have created. There is little incentive, now, for heads to move on to second headships or elsewhere. Time for short-term contracts, possibly, or a fundamental change in the career structure within education? Could we not have planned transfer of people between schools, administration, teacher training and research and development for the benefit of all these areas?

One thing I think would work for the good of the whole profession would be an appraisal programme for teachers. Though times have changed a little we are still too cosy and too quick to reject even positive criticism. Pupils have only one chance at education. If their experiences are poor because of bad teaching, it reflects upon us all. We have a poor public image at the moment, and it's time we opened ourselves up much more to scrutiny.

The life of a head or a deputy head would be improved beyond measure if we had much more administrative support. Managers need to be creative and to spend their time with people, not paper. A large school, like any other large organization, needs accountants, site managers, health and safety and transport officers, a nurse and powerful technological back-up for all administrative processes. Teacher associations are quite rightly protective of teachers' jobs, but it's unfortunate when this muddles the division that clearly exists between the administration of the school and the teaching, and turns talented teachers into book-keepers so they feel they have no time to do effectively what they are paid to do.

If we can't get rid of schools let's at least make sure that those who teach in them are as effective as they can be, for the benefit of the pupils who are all our future.

Commentary

Alston raises a number of important issues. First, what schools can learn about management and organization from industry. While accepting the use of business terminology ('targets', 'performance indicators' and 'audits'), some might question the inference that British industrial management is sufficiently successful to provide an appropriate model for schools to emulate. The received wisdom is that the prevalent style of industrial

management is, in too many cases, far removed from Alston's commendable participatory model, with its 'shared vision' and 'shared ownership'.

Second, he raises challenging issues – especially pertinent at this time of
change – about making large, inflexible institutions responsive to individuals' needs. At the same time, he stresses the need for analysis of how
learning takes place and how quality, coherence and progression in
achievement can be promoted. These issues, always present, have assumed
a greater prominence with the introduction of the National Curriculum.

Third, Alston, like subsequent contributors, draws attention to low
teacher morale. While members of the profession suffer from low pay and
low public esteem they are, Alston argues, a school's most valuable resource. As such, teachers need to be given responsibilities and the opportunity to contribute to decision-making. They also need to feel valued and
to be rewarded.

Fourth, he questions what incentives there are for headteachers to move
to another school. This is a difficult issue for any established headteacher.
It is a point echoed by Flecknoe (Chapter 3). In other systems headteachers can be transferred between schools or into administrative posts.
This can be a mixed blessing but does provide greater opportunities both
for individual headteachers and for aspiring heads.

2
Pat Collings
Sinfin Community School

Pat Collings was born and brought up in Shropshire, the third in a family of four girls. She was educated at Madeley Methodist Controlled School, Coalbrookdale County High School and at the University of Hull, where she read French with Swedish, and spent a year in France as an assistante. *She gained a first-class honours degree in 1963 and married the same year. Her first post was as a part-time teacher introducing French in two Hull primary schools. Raising a daughter and a son over the next eight years was combined with a range of part-time posts in secondary schools covering the full age and ability range in Hull, the Wirral and Nottingham. Her first full-time appointment was to Chilwell Comprehensive School, Nottingham, when it opened in 1972. Here her career developed with posts of responsibility in both the pastoral and academic structure until her appointment as deputy head at Rushcliffe Comprehensive School, West Bridgford, in January 1980. In April 1984 she took up her present post as head of Sinfin Community School, Derby. She is a trustee of the Central Bureau for Educational Visits and Exchanges and a member of the Council of the Secondary Heads Association and, currently, is seconded to the LEA as one of its appraisal project co-ordinators.*

THE SCHOOL

Sinfin Community School was opened in 1974 as a new school serving a sector of Derby city and Stenson Fields Parish in South Derbyshire, but it was designed primarily to serve a new housing development to the south of

21

an old housing estate built in 1935. Initially the LEA was Derby Borough Council; during the building period Derbyshire County Council became the LEA responsible for the school.

The school was to have been purpose built for an 11–18 intake but plans were shelved during the school's construction and the final phase of the building was never completed. Larger classes of 11–16-year-olds in, for example, the block originally intended for sixth form use (which now houses the humanities suite) cause some accommodation problems. The school's external design is pleasing and includes a well-planted courtyard area, maturing trees in grassy banks and extensive playing fields. Community provision includes the Moorlands Youth Club, which meets in the school in the evenings. The daytime and evening community programme brings over 1,000 additional users to the school, from 'Tumbletots' (pre-school gymnastics) and their parents, to a social-services day centre for elderly house-bound people and a growing number of adults who join students in timetabled daytime classes.

Since the re-organization of Derby's secondary schools, pupils normally transfer only from the five local primary schools, though some pupils from the inner city make special application to come to Sinfin Community School to join their siblings. As the Sinfin area enters into a further phase of expansion, projected numbers are expected to rise from the current 880 to reach 1,000 by 1993. Students continue their education in the new Derby tertiary colleges.

In recent years the former Sherwood Forresters' Barracks site just 2½ miles up the road has been developed as a leisure complex complete with multiscreen cinema, hotel, bowling and drive-through fast-food outlet. Meanwhile the school remains the only provider of out-of-school activity in the immediate neighbourhood (but it is an inconvenient bus ride away from Old Sinfin) both for young people and for adults who want to supplement the social club, the pubs or the churches. The shopping centre, known as the Sinfin Centre, is just that: the superstore has changed hands between national chains four times in the last six years and the remaining small shops, pubs, library, health centre and fish and chip shop all suffer from regular vandalism. The design contributes to the general air of dowdiness, despite efforts carried out jointly with the school to clean up the environment. A bright mural covers one wall opposite the Sinfin library, which was' painted by members of the youth club and of Derby Community Arts. It is also subject to graffiti. A busy road separates this centre from the school and large quantities of litter from the centre blow onto the school site and lodge in the boundary hedges. Residents regularly write to the council asking for better maintenance of their local centre.

The area has a relatively mobile population since many homes are cheap compared with the rest of Derby, and young families tend to move on. This, combined with a number of particularly vulnerable socially deprived people, who are mobile for very different reasons (e.g. housing problems or marital breakdown), means that the school may have a turnover of approximately one tenth of its population in any one year.

While the school undoubtedly has a full range of ability in its intake, tests administered in year 6 indicate that there is a skew towards the less able. About 20 children are statemented under the Education Act 1981 and there are about 30 for whom English-language support is essential. Approximately 20 per cent of the students overall are from ethnic-minority families, mainly from Pakistani, Muslim or Punjabi Sikh backgrounds. A small number of Afro-Caribbean families are represented.

While the new owner-occupied housing brings reasonably prosperous families to the area, Old Sinfin remains a pocket of significant economic and social disadvantage. This is confirmed by social services and the police, whose services are under constant pressure. Many children entering the infant departments of two partner primary schools lack basic social and language skills. The recent expansion of nursery education, together with increasing community provision for young mothers and toddlers, is designed to combat the educational disadvantage of those children whose difficulties are still apparent at secondary school. A small number of aspiring middle-class parents move deliberately to adjoining suburbs to seek access to comprehensive schools with a record of high academic achievement.

Work designed to support Old Sinfin community initiatives has a high priority in our community programme, while the LEA staffing formula (based on free-meal take-up) currently provides an enhancement of 5.4 staff to counter social deprivation. There is also a staffing supplement for all-ability teaching, which is the norm throughout the school, and a further supplement for personal and social education that, at Sinfin, is delivered mainly through a structured tutorial programme and modular courses in years 10 and 11. The Derbyshire Education for All service provides staff for community language teaching in Urdu and Punjabi, support for bilingual pupils and an Afro-Caribbean support teacher who works alongside colleagues in the mathematics team.

The school became one of three pilot schools for community education in Derbyshire in 1983, attracting an additional allowance and two extra staff. There is a thriving community-education programme that takes place on and off site in the daytime, evening, at weekends and during school holidays. Many of the 68 teaching staff are also tutors on this programme

and three additional members of staff have joint school and community
contracts.

PERSONAL PHILOSOPHY OF EDUCATION

My own life experience as a school pupil, student, parent, teacher and adult
learner have all informed my philosophy and practice in education, much
more directly than any reading or training. As a child I learnt easily and
appeared to have few problems in achieving consistently high standards in
all my school work, including examinations. However, I was extremely
sensitive and had a vivid imagination. *I* saw myself as a failure, and successes did nothing to convince me otherwise: they were flukes! After all,
hadn't I failed the 11-plus examination on the first occasion? It was only in
adult life that I recognized I had been entered for that examination aged
9½ and not awarded the place on these grounds alone! This initial experience, along with a few embarrassing exposures in the classroom at grammar school, made an indelible mark. If some of my most formative
experiences had been the relatively few negative ones, how much more so
must it be true for children labelled 'non-academic' or 'under-achievers'?

Similarly my own children had no major learning difficulties, but I shall
always remember when a teacher's emphasis on neatness unwittingly
stifled creative writing for my son, then aged 7. Hence my wholehearted
commitment to educational provision based on opportunities for *success*
for all children. One of my sisters is mentally handicapped and I was very
close to the taunts and cruel laughter her disability attracted in childhood.
My belief in the individual's right to be respected and to be offered appropriate learning programmes undoubtedly stems in part from such deep
personal experiences, as does my commitment to community education
and to learning programmes that respond to needs identified by using
formal and informal assessment methods. I see community education as an
'umbrella' that shelters pastoral care, support for learning, equal opportunities and education for a pluralist society. My commitment to community education has been fostered by my own pleasure in learning in the
informal setting of a community programme. For example, for two years I
was excited by the new skills I tried to acquire, along with other learners of
all ages, in silver-smithing classes. Some of my most touching moments as a
head have been when adult learners, who missed out during their statutory
period of education, have talked about the delights of learning alongside
14- and 15-year-olds. While ultimately the enrichment of learning for
young people has to be our priority in school, I see this as entirely

compatible with the provision of a programme that facilitates interaction between different age-groups and ethnic groups in the community so that the school is a less artificial environment than it might be. Outside school, people learn in mixed age-groups; good teachers learn with, and from, their students. I am committed to the notion of learning *with* rather than *from* and see all experiences as having potential for rich learning. In personal terms this has meant learning and developing through parenting, coping with family crises, home management, living in another country, new sporting and arts activities and informal discussion, as much as through formal learning and professional experiences. I am, quite simply, fascinated by the learning process.

My training as a modern linguist led me to value language learning for the additional skills it brings to the individual but, most importantly, for its potential to enhance understanding of the cultural links between concept and expression. The acquisition of a second language can be the beginning of world citizenship and a key to self-knowledge. This deeply held conviction informs my approach to bilingualism in the Asian and Afro-Caribbean communities – I take every opportunity to undermine the deficit model that equates inadequate English with limited academic potential and to harness resources for language support. The principles that underpin my work are entitlement, respect and equal worth.

Students are entitled to free education and to learning experiences that value heritage and cultural background but that also prepare for tomorrow and an unknown future. Access to continuing education, formal or informal, follows on naturally. The most important learning is for living. Respect for the individual and for the individual as a member of a group, whether that group be by race, gender, age, family, friendship, ethnic origin or mother tongue, is crucial. Educational practice should give equal worth to the affective and the cognitive and to *how* as well as to *what* to learn.

Human fallibility is a natural phenomenon that applies to children, parents, teachers, headteachers and other professionals. Advocating learning from mistakes has to apply to us all. I see in my role the need to articulate clear principles and to set parameters within which staff feel they can operate freely and expect me to carry the can!

On arrival as the new head at Sinfin Community School I found a strange mismatch between the philosophy as outlined in the literature and my early observation of how it was for students in a 'community school'. Locked doors, grubby notices declaring 'No dogs, No bicycles' liberally displayed around the school, the lack of basic provisions in the toilets, the lack of challenge to race or gender stereotypes in the displays all seemed out of tune with a community approach.

The message to staff from my predecessor had been that the school was 'light years ahead', and so my most difficult task of raising awareness of the need for change began. It was not a school where classroom visiting was seen as a threat and I enjoyed opportunities to see good teaching in action and to assess where allies for change might be found. I also found the monitoring of language used in public documents and letters going out through the school office a way of demonstrating my principles in practice. In addition, unless a parent or child requested to see me alone, the tutor or classteacher or team leader saw me in action with parents and pupils and during the information-giving session for short-listed candidates for teaching posts.

ORGANIZATION AND MANAGEMENT

The structure of the school is designed to create teams of staff in specialist and related curriculum areas and to encourage overlap between pastoral, academic and community interests. All three deputy headteachers have oversight of a pastoral 'section' of the school and their responsibilities include liaison with primary schools (in the year-7 team) and with employers and post-16 education (in the years 10–11 section).

The curriculum is managed by team leaders responsible to one of the three senior teachers. The six curriculum areas managed by team leaders are mathematics, science, technology, English, humanities and languages. Cross-curricular responsibilities are carried by co-ordinators of equal opportunities (gender), careers, information technology, examinations, Technical and Vocational Education (TVE), learning support and health-related fitness. Six of the assistant team leaders carry joint responsibility for supporting a curriculum area along with a pastoral support role. These posts were created to provide the broadest possible introduction to management roles and have proved very successful. Since music and drama have a whole-school role and community dimension, these areas are allocated the same allowance as assistant team leaders but without the pastoral support role.

In practice I recognize the need to use a range of decision-making styles depending on the potential repercussions of the proposed change. I have tried to put in place meetings structures that foster participation in decision-making by as many staff as possible. The meetings structure illustrates the interaction between the various groups.

Arrangements for meetings during teachers' contracted time are based on the various teams, though there are always more groups wishing to consult than time available to accommodate them. I meet formally with the deputies on a weekly basis and the community tutor joins this meeting for most of the business. We are now extending the membership to include the senior teachers as their role has become more clearly identified with the senior team.

In principle, tutors stay with their group throughout the school; for a time we re-organized year 9 from seven to ten groups on transfer to year 10, in recognition of the heavy tutorial demands on staff. This year we have reverted to the continuity of groups, which is preferred by tutors, parents and pupils. The investment of time in building relationships has begun to bear fruit. At Sinfin the tutor is the first point of reference for a parent or for a pupil seeking guidance. A weekly timetabled tutorial period delivers a programme of support for learning, ranging from getting to know the school and its expectations on entry to preparation for work experience in year 10. Learning groups based on the tutor group are the norm.

During my first unforgettable term in the summer of 1984, teacher availability for consultation was haphazard at best: all after-school activities were hit by the teacher action. When the LEA invited schools to bid for inclusion in their secondary development project, I jumped at the opportunity to attract resources that enabled groups of staff to meet during the school day (no teacher union objected to this). The project brief was to devise and to try out strategies for school improvement, focusing on the curriculum and the environment for learning, with a view to minimizing disruptive behaviour. A spate of student exclusions before I arrived helped our case for selection. The deputies were supportive, the bid went off and we became one of the first six schools to take part in this venture.

For five years a school action team led by a deputy head has managed this project. The membership has changed but has always included a member of staff in their first or second year of teaching and women have usually been in the majority. Members decide on methods of assessing school needs (surveys, interviews, action research in classrooms have all played a part in this) allocate the time, manage the working groups and disseminate findings both in school and between other project schools. They have also run sessions at weekend conferences, which have attracted much interest. A host of working groups have provided a model of delegation that has successfully counteracted the inevitable hierarchical structure. The project, in the early stages, was a rich source of learning about delegation for me personally, as well as for the deputy and her team. We agreed to approach eight members of teaching staff who, we felt, represented a balance of the staff using as criteria length of service, seniority, gender, curriculum and pastoral responsibilities. We took care to include influential staff who were fairly vociferous in resisting the changes expected as a result of my appointment. This method of team composition proved to be a mistake – they struggled! Interestingly, the process of building a team whose members would have preferred to be told what to do and how to do it, rather than to identify their own task, seemed to mirror what was happening in the rest of the school. Having arrived in April at the onset of the teachers' national dispute, I used the existing meeting structure for the summer and autumn terms and suggested that a review of school aims would be appropriate with the arrival of a new head. Once again the combination of their low morale, lack of confidence and an understandable uncertainty as to exactly where I stood (and perhaps a belief that it was the head's job to produce policy documents anyway) resulted in bemusement rather than action.

Five project years later I hope and believe that the way in which the school action team works now is illustrative of a greater trust in the process of delegation by me and of the expertise of many more staff in recognizing the importance of that process. The first team eventually gave birth painfully to our school guidelines. Despite a mutually agreed move to positive rather than negative student-behaviour guidelines (e.g. 'move quietly' rather than 'don't run') and the clear advice of the deputy, the group's proposals arrived with 'obey all instructions given by teachers'. I could not feel comfortable supporting the word 'obey' but more important, perhaps, I recognized the hurt experienced by teachers who felt real ownership of their work at this stage.

The guidelines eventually read 'Follow all instructions given by teachers'. I learnt to monitor progress regularly and intervene if necessary, well before the final draft of proposals. I have since tried to set parameters within which groups are given the authority to operate, making and learning from their own mistakes wherever possible. The secondary development project has managed the setting up of increasingly flexible working groups who have engaged in activities as diverse as action research, teacher tracking, monitoring gender bias, classroom support, display and environmental improvements. Bids for time in which to do a piece of work always exceed the time available, despite the need for teachers to do yet more preparatory and follow-up work.

STAFFING STRUCTURE

As a school for 11–16-year-olds in an expanding area of Derby, Sinfin Community School, along with three other Derby schools, was not

included in the post-primary review of education that led to the establishment of tertiary colleges, the closure of schools and the establishment of
'new' schools, which opened in September 1989. Our staffing was seriously
affected, however, as posts were subjected to temporary contracts for a
period of two years and held over for possible redeployments from the
Derby schools in the re-organization. Sadly, the teacher unions who had
been signatories to the county agreement had not foreseen the consequences for schools such as ours. In the event, we started the new school
year in September 1989 with twelve new teachers, only four of whom came
through redeployment. Filling the temporary vacancies was a recurring
nightmare and occupied a disproportionate amount of management and
administration time. We provided induction programmes for some excellent new teachers only to see them move on before our posts were released
from the constraints of being held in a central pool intended to accommodate teachers not placed in the re-organized schools. The near coincidence
with the new pay and conditions of service (1987) led to complexities
unique to Sinfin Community School and there was no easy way out of
them.

For years the school had been generously staffed by the LEA through a
series of compensatory or developmental staffing policies. In particular, in
1987, using a free-meals indicator for social deprivation, an additional 6.8
teachers came our way. We already had two community tutors and four
section-11 posts in our establishment (all of these have since been counted
as supplementary to establishment) and named special-needs teachers supporting pupils for the specified number of hours on their statement of
learning needs. Our all-ability groupings and growing programme of personal and social education has also brought teaching-staff supplements. In
vain I pleaded for appropriate scale posts, non-teaching support and resource backing in exchange for some of this staffing supplement. Delighted
as we were to be able to indulge in some innovatory staffing (for example,
an outdoor-pursuits teacher on a flexible contract and a second music
teacher with time allocated to primary liaison) we all recognized the additional strain on space (smaller groups need more rooms), middle managers
and the already over-stretched budget for basic school books and equipment. The advent of financial delegation may eventually rectify such problems but the legacy of this generosity was a decidedly skewed management
structure. While most schools had experienced falling roles and were strug-
gling to *reduce* their number of allowances, the new pay structure in the
first year alone brought us 22 new internal promotion opportunities!

I never did find another head managing expansion on this scale but
found the need for just as much sensitivity as in the reduction of

allowances, in an exercise where there was actually more *dis*appointment than appointment. It had been essential to move to the new structure with the full backing of the whole staff. Numerous fascinating contributions to the debate led us, eventually, to a structure that is adjusted annually and that led HMI, in the report of their visit in October 1989, to declare that the school is well placed to deliver the National Curriculum.

I have always been determined to retain an integrated management structure for community education within Sinfin Community School. Ironically, when a new, major, county initiative came on line to extend access to community education to everyone in the county (with *every* school available as a community education base) this posed a threat to our integrated model. The establishment of a new bureaucracy created real tensions, particularly for existing school-based community tutors who found themselves being managed by their local community-education officer as well as by their head. With the advent of the local management of schools (LMS) further potential for dividing school and community provision is inevitable, but we remain determined to hang on to what we know to be worth preserving.

The inspection by HMI in the autumn term 1989 certainly helped us to focus on our strengths and weaknesses although there were no major surprises. We were pleased that the inspection team noted the efforts of hard-working staff giving strong pastoral support to their students who, as a result, feel secure at school and enjoy good classroom relationships. Positive community links and open access were praised. School documentation was described as excellent. The published report stressed the need for teachers to give students greater challenge and to expect more creative and reflective responses from them. The inspection team highlighted good management and communication and clear statements of policy and philosophy but reported that these were not uniformly reflected in the classroom.

The short inspection confirmed me in the view that the independence of HMI is both its strength and its weakness. The nature of these inspections means that resident expertise in evaluating the school can only be used in the gathering of the data required. It was personally very rewarding to be able to share perceptions with the reporting inspector on an informal basis and I thoroughly enjoyed our daily exchanges. The fact that I had been one of the group of British headteachers and LEA officers and advisers on a study visit to New York in October 1988, working alongside HMI, obviously gave me an insider's view of the process of inspection. I felt able to prepare the school for the visit and viewed it as a unique opportunity for external assessment and professional development for me. It is a rare experience for a head to receive professional reflections on the detail of the school by a third party. Despite the inevitable anxieties and disruption, I believe the benefits of the inspection were far greater than the sum total of all the LEA versions of inspection to which we had been party over the years. The governing body had confirmation of our successes and of those areas that were of concern to them. For classteachers, I believe that the effectiveness of any observation depended on the relationship established between the observer and observed during the classroom visit – reflections or recommendations were embraced willingly when sensitively given.

Forearmed by the experience of other heads, I prepared a press statement to be released on publication of the report. The subsequent favourable press cuttings have been well used, although I was uncomfortable with the removal of all but the positive points by the LEA press office. An action plan was drawn up based on the report's findings and I believe that many necessary changes were assisted or speeded up significantly as a result of the inspection. It certainly made me more confident in the monitoring role and gave weight to the case for raising expectations of the pupils and further support to the work of the school action team.

In the current economic climate it is not surprising that our 'charge-capped' authority has not jumped in with the recommended new library or refurbishment of the drama space! None the less, the governing body has used the report to highlight these needs once again. It was a useful experience overall but could, I believe, have been even more effective had the inspection team been constructed after a preliminary visit to the school.

ORGANIZATION AND MANAGEMENT OF LEARNING

As with the arrival of the GCSE in 1988, the apparent demands of the National Curriculum, in terms of organization and management of our curriculum, did not appear too daunting. We were well placed to deliver the broad, balanced curriculum both in the lower school and at 14 years plus. We had already taken steps to ensure a programme of balanced science for all students with a humanities subject, and an expressive arts subject, as well as English, mathematics, careers and personal development and physical and religious education. Our plan for TVE included a language for all by 1991–2 and take-up of the language option was already increasing. The impetus for change had come from planning for TVE and from our insistence on balance and equity in all children's programmes. We accept setting by ability only after year 8 in the linear subjects, such as languages and mathematics. All subjects, including health-related fitness, are taught in mixed-sex groups. The National Curriculum requirements certainly added credibility and speed to our proposed developments. The amount of time devoted to valuable non-examination work, however, was at first seen to be under considerable threat, despite our own growing confidence in the work done in tutorial time and in the careers and personal-development slot.

The arrival of the orders for National Curriculum technology imposed change in a curriculum area where we knew there was a real need for it. The solution had to be worked out in the areas concerned. The new structure should result in the acquisition of technological skills alongside truly open-ended design tasks. Funding, of course, is inadequate: self-help has been the only way of adapting the space available for craft, design and technology to permit access to computing and electronics.

We have prepared for the potential overload at key-stage 4 (which at the time of writing appears to be being renegotiated) by adjusting to a six-period day. Despite the National Curriculum, I am determined not to see the expressive arts take a subordinate role. In terms of increasing confidence, self-knowledge and opportunity for success, they enhance the quality of life so much, particularly for young people who may not have access to the arts in their home lives other than through television.

In mathematics and science the National Curriculum has provided a welcome, though demanding, formal structure for collaboration with our partner primary schools to ensure a recording system designed to provide the maximum up-to-date information with minimal administration for teachers. Finding time for the essential meetings after school has not been easy, mindful as we are of the enormous burden on our primary colleagues who have had to adapt their work schemes and acquire new expertise in such a short time.

At Sinfin, pupils with special educational needs are fully integrated into mainstream work. Withdrawal is exceptional and reserved for special short programmes to tackle specific learning problems after consultation with the classteacher, parents and the pupil. Since approximately 20 per cent of any group need some learning support, individual links with curriculum areas have been developed and a support teacher is deployed to operate as a member of that curriculum team. He or she offers support in the classroom alongside the specialist but takes the lead role from time to time, and assists with preparation and monitoring of materials and equipment, as well as recording progress and consulting the pupil's tutor. Language-support teachers are similarly deployed, with the result that many pupils are able to seek help from one of a team of teachers without that support being specifically labelled. This flexibility makes great demands on the support teacher but any stigma attached to receiving 'extra help' is significantly diminished. We are all aware that we are still working *towards* effective differentiation in the classroom. No one is yet satisfied but our teachers are, without exception, eager to grapple with the problem.

At Sinfin nowhere is differentiation more necessary or more difficult than in the setting of tasks for homework. The more imaginative task may make unrealistic demands of our pupils who may be attending Koranic schools, minding younger children or be unable to find a willing adult to interview or assist with the gathering of information. There is an ever-present dilemma between rigour and reasonable expectation, with a growing recognition by teachers that to 'excuse' the task is to deny the opportunity.

RELATIONSHIPS

During my introduction to candidates for any post on their interview day I always stress the importance of internal staff relationships, highlighting membership of various staff groupings. Until compulsory competitive tendering removed the cleaning staff from direct management by the school, any new appointee was included in the total staff group, which numbered just under two hundred. Because of the times of working sessions, contracts and loyalties, this large group cannot meet in full and the immediate departmental team is seen as the main source of support. I try to facilitate inclusion rather than exclusion. Our staff handbook lists all permanent staff alphabetically (whether teaching or non-teaching) and the daily staff bulletin has an informal style and the widest possible circulation with a reference point on the noticeboard for part-time or temporary staff. It has contributions from all staff sources collected by a deputy head and includes notices for students to be selected by the tutor. The only references to named students invite teachers to contact a tutor for essential confidential information relating to that student. This may be to inform teachers, where the student or parents wish the facts to be known, of the death of a grandparent, birth of a baby, break up of a marriage, court case or pregnancy, so that school can be extra sensitive to needs at such times.

Although a small number of staff were resistant to this change in my early days, we have an established first-names policy between all staff and a staff-room where visitors are welcome and where teaching and non-teaching staff can enjoy a brief break together. Inevitably, essential student news relating to absence because of exclusion or medical or disciplinary grounds is posted in the staff-room from time to time. This has never caused problems of confidentiality; non-teaching staff are trusted to show the same respect for such information as their teaching colleagues.

Midday supervisors who are in school for just over an hour each day but whose role in informal education is, I believe, as significant as a teacher's, are inducted into the school style: appropriate ways of addressing students, coping strategies when confrontation looms, avoiding gender stereotypes (for example, in the dining queue), ensuring tutor and parent contact for praise or reprimand or when injury occurs.

The role of the head at the interface with the community can be experienced in the school itself. Frequent contact with the non-teaching part-time staff who, after all, are the best ambassadors for the school in its own community, brings a tangible mutual respect. I do not under-estimate the value of their contribution – for a 'dinner-lady' to 'tell it as it is' when a damaging rumour is about is far more effective than anything I can say. I try to keep track of staff on a personal basis and don't like to miss sending a card to mark weddings, births, serious illness, bereavements or departures.

Where parents are concerned, I start from the principle that school has to overcome the historical and cultural barrier created by personal experience or social myth. At Sinfin Community School reception staff (all parents themselves) are briefed to handle parental requests sensitively in person or by telephone and are adept at recognizing the sort of distress that requires an immediate response from me or a deputy. I value the office's contribution to parent partnership most highly. The welcoming style extends to notices and the tone of letters, which are translated into Punjabi and Urdu when appropriate. I keep a continuous watching brief to maintain standards in this vital area.

Similarly our home–school liaison policy is something I reinforce constantly both at meetings to introduce the school to new parents and during less-informal admission interviews throughout the year. Teachers are given training in listening to parents during the induction programme. Regular parent contact is delegated to tutors and I am delighted that I am now most frequently consulted in an advisory capacity when the tutor or the team leader identifies the need, rather than being the first port of call. A number of tutors have called informal evening meetings for the parents of their group, even though others remain anxious or unsure of the value of this initiative. There is now sufficient skill and support to build such time into the teacher year.

During a discussion on the identification of the client in statutory education, our wise Chief Education Officer once stressed the need for heads to maintain their role as educators of the parent body and community, while genuinely listening to articulated local concerns. I have found this a useful guideline and try to keep parents informed of major school and national changes through the monthly school newsletter and occasional more formal letters.

I see parents as educational consultants to the school on entry, when discussing settling-in matters in years 7 and 10, or when considering the choice of courses and career in year 9. I try to encourage consultation procedures that reflect this. I ask a small band of parent helpers for their reaction, ideas and opinions on school literature and changes in school policy that affect them.

Recruitment and Staff Development

I see our selection procedure for appointment as a preliminary to the staff development programme that starts with induction. The literature sent out to would-be applicants, along with job description and personnel specification, is intended to exemplify our style and gives what I hope are strong pointers to our philosophy and practice. Candidates are informed that our management structure is not equitable in terms of gender balance and that ethnic minorities are under-represented. Until the governing body has control of advertisements we both benefit and are constrained by LEA advertising policy, even as to which press group to use. While restricted advertising is understood in terms of safeguarding teachers in a local authority which has a no-redundancy policy, it is extremely frustrating in practice and has been one of the greatest hindrances to the effective management of staff selection for me, particularly when applicants are in such short supply and sometimes non-existent.

In the rush to appoint before deadlines, in exceptional circumstances we have departed from our best practice on the interview day. The day is planned to give candidates maximum opportunity to decide to remain firm candidates and there are no recriminations if, as on rare occasions, they choose not to present themselves for formal interview in the afternoon. I encourage them to talk with pupils, non-teachers and other adults in and about the school, as well as during a full 'guided tour'. At interview we follow equal-opportunities procedures to the letter and 'loaded' questions are disallowed. I have used the interview for the benefit of middle managers who are included on the panel to further their own interviewing skills and to establish their future role in supporting the new member of their team. Some governors (other than the chair, who never misses an interview) are not readily available for interview panels at Sinfin but find the

experience enlightening when they can come. We always offer a debriefing
to unsuccessful candidates (internal and external) after interview and, although I never get used to, or like telling someone they have been unsuccessful, invariably I draw much satisfaction from being able to debrief on
all the strengths of the candidate, as well as the elements that did not result
in a match with our post. Indeed, I have received some most memorable
expressions of thanks for these debriefings (and the rare outburst from
someone whom I was then glad not to have appointed).

I set great store by our formal induction programme, which includes at
least one day prior to taking up the post (three for newly qualified
teachers) and a series of after-school sessions designed to cover the needs
identified by the newcomers, as well as the elements we wish to include.
They are usually not dissimilar. For example, bilingualism, equal opportunities in practice and reporting procedures come from both lists. As the
individuals get to know each other quite well, another non-hierarchical
support group is born. Over the years I have watched these very varied
groups, which include promoted post-holders, redeployed and part-time
staff, often with newly qualified teachers in the majority. They soon gain an
identity within the staff as a group. Again the expertise within the group
itself frequently provides all that is necessary and it is a pleasure to facilitate such a group. The development programme also gives other members
of staff opportunities to organize and deliver an in-service education and
training (INSET) session. This is now established practice and, I think,
seen as something of an honour!

In my time at Sinfin, staff development has shifted radically from a
laissez-faire model (the development of the willing), via TRIST (in-service
training directly linked to the early phase of TVEI), to a programme resulting from needs-based planning at the institutional and area level, altogether a more healthy state of affairs since it has greater potential to
effect change for all pupils. While this comes from the national conditions
attached to the education support grant for training, it has been matched
by attitudinal changes within the school and has not stifled interesting
initiatives.

An experiential approach to training is the norm, as is the encouragement through time allocation to self-generated working groups. When staff
are being asked to ensure that the students take an active role in their own
learning and assessment it would be inconsistent not to encourage staff to
identify their own priorities within agreed targets for the school.

The new conditions of service imposed five in-service training days over
the school year and were seen initially as part of the whole unpopular
package. Few visiting speakers who contributed to our early whole-school

closure days were greeted without scepticism and, over the three years since their introduction, our most successful events have undoubtedly been those that rely on existing expertise in our own staff. These have included skills workshops (computing, drama), community education, equal opportunities and cross-curricular issues. Small-scale pieces of work, involving pairs of teachers or small groups to pursue a specific task with a clear purpose in a set time during the school day, is another way in which we hope to use the funding more flexibly and more effectively than in the past. More unusual opportunities have sometimes been of even greater benefit to the school than originally envisaged (for example, hosting a visiting teacher from China and post-to-post exchanges with Danish colleagues have genuinely enriched the students' understanding of linguistic and cultural similarities as well as of differences, which can then be celebrated).

As head I am a 'networker', putting areas of good practice in touch with each other. There is genuine delight when teachers share their successes and working practices with each other – discussing an exhibition of work put together for an equal-opportunities in-service event, for example, or simply telling others of recent initiatives in a brief presentation.

Appraisal

There was already an annual, individual, interview system for teaching staff when I arrived. The interview was conducted and recorded by the head and the outcome noted was invariably a suggested further qualification, course or promotion route. Despite the unhealthy climate of industrial action, I was very keen to build on this system and moved it forward to a prepared self-appraisal to be conducted and recorded by me. I introduced this on a voluntary basis, offering the opportunity to about 25 staff. I struggled to find the time for all who took up the offer but thoroughly enjoyed listening to teachers reflecting on their work with the aid of the simple prompts I had provided in advance. As a result of this work, a seconded head researching into appraisal systems used Sinfin for his study and this, I suspect, kept my project going! His report was very positive but, after two years, it became abundantly clear that one person could not carry the load alone and, in any event, I wanted the skills of appraising and being appraised to be more widely acquired and used. The deputies were already involved; senior teachers were given brief and somewhat inadequate training but now run their own embryonic systems over the whole year. We plan to move on to classroom observation and recording skills and to ensure that appraisal is integrated with staff development.

I am convinced that developmental appraisal is a professional entitlement. As with previous stages of our developing appraisal scheme, all the professional association representatives will be consulted. I have found it very helpful to seek their opinions early in such matters and have regretted those occasions when something has delayed the crucial moment for consultation. During sensitive staff-disciplinary hearings I have always valued the presence of professional representatives since our mutual aim is to put matters right. On occasions, however, our different priorities have led to tensions, making life uncomfortable for a while.

Governing Body

Since the school serves an area where local people, in general, are not queueing up to become members of school governing bodies, the requirement (under the Education Act 1986) for greater parent representation was welcomed by me. As a group, our parent-governors have welcomed training and other opportunities to visit the school in the working day. The demands made on governors who are working parents by the Education Reform Act 1988 (ERA) are unrealistic, but ours have had an excellent attendance record at meetings of the governing body and their commitment to the students is never in doubt. For tireless dedication I have to single out the chairman of governors who has remained in the chair since my appointment. Neither of us found it easy to build a working relationship in the early days as it was difficult for an observer to distinguish the effects of a new head from the effects of industrial action. We now agree on an open style that allows occasional 'mistakes' on either side to be dealt with promptly. Having served as a county councillor, he is extremely well versed in procedure and has supported me in encouraging governors to undertake structured visits to school, to take a special interest in, say, pupils' induction to school, and to accompany me on joint LMS training initiatives.

Relationships with the wider community follow naturally from the governing body, on which Rolls-Royce, a major employer in Derby, is well represented. I have spent a considerable time visiting all the major local employers and many hours preparing for the compact which did not, in the end, come to fruition. Our major school links with local commerce and industry come from the annual work-experience programme, while small-scale sponsorship for our school brochure's new glossy folder was successfully acquired last year by the deputy head. This prospectus was a planned change but was given additional impetus by the need for higher profile marketing in the wake of ERA.

I do not wish to see the new marketing initiatives as anything other than a sharpening of good practice that puts clear, well-presented information before parents. With schools currently considered to blame for all the nation's ills, the highlighting of success and achievement in schools is, I believe, a matter of professional integrity.

While I have not always been successful in gaining media coverage for school plays or fund-raising initiatives, the school has featured on radio and in several television productions. One programme followed five school-leavers through their preparation for life beyond school. It was a fascinating experience for the students and staff involved, including me. More recently a Leicester headteacher and I were filmed in our own schools and in New York by the BBC as we took part in the HMI study visit.

PERSONAL REFLECTIONS

Headship has been challenging and has given me opportunities to extend myself and to gain real fulfilment. However, all challenging and fulfilling jobs have their downs, and headship is no exception.

I was never more conscious of sexism in the profession and in society than when I first became a head. Never before had I been consistently addressed as 'sir' in letters, mistaken for a secretary or presumed not to be able to deal easily with misbehaving teenage boys. I actually kept a record (a little blue book) of the examples of offensive behaviour and language for the first three years. My awareness of the need to address gender issues more urgently in the classroom sprang from this and was inextricably linked to equal-opportunities issues for young people from ethnic-minority groups. For a black female student or teacher, sexism is but another layer of prejudice to overcome. It is certainly not enough simply to hope that the role model of a female head will in itself effect change in the experiences of girls and other women in the school. In this respect I have been very fortunate in being able to support work in the school initiated by others committed to the cause, but have made it part of my role to keep equal opportunities high on the agenda in and out of school; as a result I have had to take care not to be labelled the feminist head!

On a more mundane level, could anyone enjoy checking out the latest vandalism or graffiti? My pet hate, however, is picking up litter though, paradoxically, I rarely miss doing it when I am in school; I wish this personal example worked to better effect.

Some of the challenging tensions of the job come from following up parental complaints that have proved to have substance. My loyalty to staff is very strong but cannot extend to whitewashing their mistakes, any more than my own. If we lose some of the mystique by admitting to human feelings I think we gain in credibility and approachability.

I am irritated by meaningless bureaucracy, especially when it requires me to ask hard-working colleagues to produce something yesterday. If there are other aspects of the job I don't like temporarily these are invariably due to the phenomenal pressure of work. The pressing time-scale of recent government-initiated change has been compounded by far too much detail and prescription. Bureaucratic inflexibility and a de-skilled teaching force are hardly a recipe for success.

Headship may possibly not be totally manageable, as there has always to be an elastic amount of time available to react to situations however well organized or well equipped the school or the head may be. However, a considerable increase in non-teaching assistance and office technology would certainly make the job more manageable. But then so would an eight-day week, or perhaps a 26-hour day!

If I had a magic wand, I would create the supportive climate for comprehensive State education in Britain that, currently, does not exist. There would be generous funding. Selection and appointment of teachers would be uncomplicated, with a good supply of well-qualified graduates in every discipline. There would be no more last-minute gap-filling, which uses management time so inefficiently.

Failing a resort to magic, what are some of the rewards? After six and a half years I am able to recognize how much I have grown in the job and become more confident in many of its demands. Headship has certainly extended me and I do feel privileged to have the overview that enables me to see and hear of so much good teaching and to have had some influence on the development of individuals and groups of teachers. I like listening to young people and watching them emerge as young men and women. On a daily basis, I value the variety of exchanges with other people (and suffer withdrawal symptoms in the first few days of a holiday). Headship is, none the less, a lonely job. Close personal support 'in-house' is rare for heads in a profession where that is the norm for everyone else. I enjoy the company of other headteachers in a professional setting and often sharpen my thinking or glean new ideas in discussion with particular friends who are also educators over a meal or on a country walk. I also enjoy giving a head's perspective in groups drawn from a wider circle – for example, at board meetings of the Central Bureau for Educational Visits and Exchanges.

My spirits are frequently raised by very simple gestures from the pupils – a smile or a wave of acknowledgement as I arrive in the morning; offers of help or brief informal exchanges in the corridor or over lunch restore my morale. The pupils are, for me, the best source of information about the quality of their learning experiences.

If I were to highlight significant periods of personal professional development leading to better understanding of my own strengths, weaknesses and potential, I would want to include my first formal appraisal as a deputy head by that school's general adviser; being a group facilitator on certain management courses; participating in an intensive Coverdale management course for heads; and being a group leader on the 1988 HMI study visit to New York. The common denominators seem to have been supportive, professional, 'critical friends' and time to reflect. Life would have been less satisfying without these experiences.

Commentary

Collings discusses three issues of direct concern to new headteachers. First, how to raise the critical awareness of long-serving staff. Establishing one's own identity as a new head in a school is always likely to be a challenge. But that challenge is greater when the existing staff group (or a significant proportion of it) considers that the school is doing well and that there is no need for change. These perceptions, based often on the achievement of what are deemed reasonable results, lie at the heart of the debate on effective schools and school improvement.

Second, Collings indicates the need to develop a range of decision-making styles along a continuum, from democratic to autocratic; an issue also addressed by other contributors. A major challenge of headship is to know which issues lie at what point along the continuum.

Similar skills are needed when it comes to delegation – Collings' third issue. Her account illustrates that the head has to tread a very narrow line between delegating so much that he or she is seen (by at least some disgruntled colleagues) to be abdicating responsibility, and between delegating so little that staff feel scant ownership of the running of the school. It is clear that learning to trust, to take risks and to accept some failures are essential elements in delegation.

Collings also raises an issue of concern to women headteachers – sexism. Despite considerable progress in many schools on equal opportunities, and despite conscious efforts by some LEAs to encourage more women into senior positions, sexism is still an issue with which female heads have to deal. For Collings, although annoying and disappointing on a personal level, the experience of sexism has had a positive spin-off in that it has strengthened her resolve to address, *in the classroom*, issues of equal opportunities and of how to deal with prejudice in relation not only to gender but also to race.

3
Mervyn Flecknoe
Carlton-Bolling College

Mervyn Flecknoe was brought up in Gedling, Nottingham. He associates his childhood with the River Trent, with Nottingham Market Square and with the Goose Fair. He attended a State school and then King's College, London. After gaining a physics degree he went to work for ICI on Teesside. There he became a leader of the Eastern Ravens Club, which aimed to befriend children from areas of poverty who were identified as being 'at risk'. This experience as a volunteer convinced him that his career lay in teaching and he subsequently gained a Post Graduate Certificate of Education at Leicester University in the heady days of 1968. Since then he has taught at Shirebrook School in Derbyshire, the Sutton Centre in Nottinghamshire and at Stantonbury Campus in Milton Keynes. He is now headteacher of Carlton-Bolling College in Bradford, West Yorkshire.

He has been married to a community development worker since 1971 and has three children. He enjoys wildlife, gardening and two-wheeled transport. He has been a member of the Methodist Church for most of his life and would claim that his attitude to education was informed by Christian beliefs, although most of his students are Muslim.

He has taken part in the HMI-inspired Teaching in the City *seminars and study visits to schools in the USA and has undertaken a research project at the University of York on the response of schools to the climate of change.*

THE SCHOOL

Carlton-Bolling is an LEA-maintained college that caters for 1,200 students in years 9–13, of whom 260 are in the 'sixth form'. There are also over

600 adult attendances in the daytime each week for activities ranging from A-level sociology to a parent and toddler group. Many adults fit into the odd spaces in sixth-form teaching groups and workshops, while others attend special courses run under the auspices of Urban Aid. Altogether 150 adults are on courses of some kind; another 100 attend clubs and activities organized by the community but that have a home in the college. All adult provision is free, including a crèche.

The buildings date from 1975 and are purpose built and carpeted. Students enter the college from many feeder middle schools; 90 per cent have Asian origins and over half have an unwritten first language. The largest group of Asian students is from Muslim families originating in Mirpur, although Sikh, Hindu and Muslim families from Bangladesh are all represented. Urdu is the main foreign language taught.

The college is in the inner city of Bradford and the majority of families cope with low socioeconomic status and poor housing conditions, while preserving their dignity and culture.

PERSONAL PHILOSOPHY OF EDUCATION

Most of our ancestors did most of their learning in villages; they learnt from people whom they respected and also from their peers. They learnt through play, through real constructive work and from the activities of family responsibility; they learnt in an environment in which they felt safe and over which their families had some control. They learnt through sitting puzzled, through individual and group activity with others of similar and of widely differing ages. In particular, they learnt from grandparents.

Our best efforts in educating teenagers so far this century have revolved around sitting them at desks in a relatively barren environment, in which they have had restricted roles and little responsibility, with only others of their own age. Frequently the teacher in charge knew little about them. Activity was taken out of learning and the relationships that are so vital were undervalued. If you ask people about their happy memories of school they will often talk about their relationship with a cherished teacher or they will tell of some co-operative exercise, such as a school play. Sitting at desks is not usually reported.

My philosophy of education is dominated by the image of the village environment and by the knowledge that systems fail and that relationships are precious. People will always try to subvert and misuse systems for their own ends, but they will generally respect relationships. They will frequently be loyal to another human being where a bond has formed when a similar constraint imposed by a system would be flouted.

I also believe that all people have unfulfilled potential, and this applies to teachers as well. I believe people work best when they are cared for not only by people but also by the system. In fact, any system must be obviously for the benefit of people if it is to be respected. This usually means that it must be simple: complexity and imposition are to be avoided. This includes six-day timetables, long lists of rules, eight-period days, bells, tannoys, clipboards, and pupils standing up when a head comes into the room.

The other major influence on learning I have not mentioned so far is the smile. Smiling is far more important than we usually suspect. It conveys to the smiled upon that all is right with the world; it says there is nothing to worry about that might interfere with learning. It says, 'I care about you, you are an all right sort of person'. Smiling is often a prelude to laughing, which should be indulged in frequently because it is a remedy for many ills, including upset stomachs, frustration, inadequate budgets and high blood pressure. Touching is also important but only when the relationship is right, so it cannot be recommended to the beginner.

The last thing to be said is that students gain little advantage by under-achieving and that schools should be places where each student is challenged constantly. This happens most wherever they are known best. The efforts of large schools to simulate close personal knowledge and to provide flexibility in learning situations in response to the needs of individuals have generally failed.

ORGANIZATION AND MANAGEMENT

One fundamental difference between Carlton-Bolling College and other secondary schools known to me is the use of the fifteen-period week. Our day begins with a 30-minute tutorial followed by three periods of 90 minutes each. At the end of the first is break; at the end of the second is lunch; and at the end of the third most students go home. The search for simplicity of organization began with this reform of the timetable. Its advantages are dramatic:

- Movement takes place when there is plenty of time for it. There is less hassle, fewer bruised shins and ruffled tempers.
- Students can get down to work without bells interrupting their concentration. They are pushed around less by the system.

- Teachers have the opportunity to forge good working relationships with their students and need these to survive.
- Lessons are long enough to accommodate most teaching and learning activities. For those that are too long, we take a fortnight in June with longer 'lessons'.

Many schools have these features in some measure by their adoption of a four-period day. The three-period day, in my view, however, is better. The National Curriculum fits well into the fifteen lessons plus tutorial. We have nine faculties of which two are support faculties and consequently not timetabled. Timetabled faculties are English, mathematics, science, languages, arts, technology and humanities. All are taught in mixed-ability groups but in languages and arts there is some choice and the teaching groups are therefore not tutor groups. In years 10 and 11 each subject has two sessions (totalling three hours), except for science, which gets three. Much of health education and careers education is dealt with in the five half-hour tutorials with which each day begins.

Mixed-ability teaching is very important in setting the atmosphere of the college. Alongside all the benefits to students, a parity of esteem is engendered among teachers. The difference in status between teachers taking the top and the bottom set is removed and it is permissible to discuss lack of success because, although teachers may have more problems teaching mixed ability, at least they all have the same problems. Mixed-ability organization makes teamwork a profitable solution to curriculum development because a good idea for one group is more likely to be transferable to other groups than under a system of setting or streaming.

Another key feature of Carlton-Bolling is the importance given to the establishment of teams, to whom a great deal of decision-making is devolved. We have tried to ensure that staff belong to only one faculty and that they do all their teaching in that faculty, preferably in their own teaching bases. The teams of tutors are almost congruent with the faculty teams. There is no reason why a group of mathematics teachers should not also make a good team of tutors in, say, year 9. Teachers whose rooms can be used for tutorial activities generally tutor in the same room in which they teach.

We have also tried to make the faculties equal in size and in esteem so that the discussions in the academic council among heads of faculty take place between equals. We have tried to make the job of tutoring important by allowing an extra non-contact period of 90 minutes for tutors. The allocation of non-contact time reflects the amount of non-teaching work that has to be performed by an individual *in teaching time*. Thus the head and two deputies receive 18 hours, year heads and faculty heads receive 9 hours and grade-B post-holders (our major promoted category) receive 4½ hours, compared with the standard allowance of 3 hours.

The senior management team meeting comprises head, two deputies and three senior teachers. Men and women are equally represented, but not, as yet, ethnic minorities (currently the highest grade held by a black or Asian teacher is the grade-C allowance). There are also frequent meetings of just the head and deputies. Having two deputies in a college that has 90 teachers even after savage cuts is much better than having three. The number of conversations one of the three senior managers must have to discuss an idea with the other two is, precisely, two. With three deputies the figure is three, an increase of 50 per cent. Adding one person to the team of three increases the communication load by half as much again. Is it worth it? It militates against corporate decision-making and leads to separation of function and to feelings of exclusion. Two deputies are also cheaper than three and the money can be spent in rewarding teachers who assume responsibility at a lower salary level. Two deputies means that other staff have more delegated to them and people seem to like this. Neither deputy has a clipboard!

The three senior teachers each have a major team-leading responsibility in addition to their senior role. The senior head of year leads a year team in addition to responsibility for students on teaching practice (a major industry). The senior head of faculty leads a faculty team in addition to responsibility for cross-curricular themes. The head of upper college (a term that embraces the 'sixth form') oversees the work of curriculum co-ordination between the sixth forms of three local schools, which comprise an organization called the East Bradford Commonwealth. Purely administrative roles are fulfilled by two people on grade-D salaries who administer the examination system and provide information, such as timetables, for staff, students and for management decision-making.

In every salary grade (counting senior teacher, head and deputy as one grade) there are roughly equal numbers of men and women. This is the result of the application of a conscious policy to ensure adequate role models for young people and to ensure that a wide spread of human experience is brought to bear on the solution of problems as they arise.

Although we have a rolling three-year plan of development, which is constantly updated by reference to the development plans of faculty and year teams, the main business of review is stimulated by the encouragement of every member of staff and student to take responsibility for events that impinge upon them and to criticize without fear of offence to dignity. This is an organic process of review and stimulus to change. It is a good system if all concerned feel able to take part. In as much as some retiring violets assume that they should not speak, that their views are known and ignored, that there is no point saying anything, the system is imperfect; but we stumble along.

Baker days are generally used for reflection. They are attached to existing holidays so that time off for students comes in complete weeks as an aid to good attendance. Staff are presented with topics on which their opinions or thoughts are required and they are asked to present the fruits of their labours when the college reconvenes. The most significant recent use of a Baker day was the creation of a mission statement:

- Education is our business.
- Students are our focus, their achievements are our reward.
- We value the cultural and religious diversity of our students, and their opinions.
- We aim to promote responsibility, caring and a love for learning.
- We provide wide and balanced educational experience.
- Our partners in this enterprise are governors, teachers, parents, commercial, industrial and voluntary organizations.

ORGANIZATION AND MANAGEMENT OF LEARNING

Over a period of eight years we have fought a constant battle to increase the amount of student activity involved in learning. This has been against a background of eleven years of reductions in expenditure on education in Bradford. Learning activities designed by teachers with little money to spend tend to be teacher led and passive experiences for the students, especially if the teachers regard themselves as the source of the information the students need in order to achieve 'education'. In a school with few books it is easy for the teachers to feel that this is true. Even when I was a student at school in the 1960s, I had a textbook for each subject. Of course that was in a grammar school and I doubt whether the same was true in the secondary-modern school down the road. Education has come a long way since then. I remember that the C-stream pupils in the grammar school were regarded as problems who did not wear uniform properly, did not do homework and who failed examinations. There were sometimes no academic expectations of secondary-modern students.

With little, if any, increase in funding in real terms, teachers have worked miracles with the advent of comprehensive schooling in bringing all students within the net of positive expectation. However, this has usually been within the same conceptual framework of the teacher as the provider of knowledge.

To convert the learning process to an active role for students in which the teacher is the enabler of learning is not an easy process. After what we thought had been a particularly successful innovation in active learning in humanities a few years ago, we took in a group of post-graduate certificate of education (PGCE) students. As a group project they studied the teaching of humanities. One of their major comments was, 'Why do you have them sitting down copying from worksheets so much?'

Active learning is messy learning in which the teacher must share the control of behaviour and of study with the students. We are gradually getting better at it. In my role as headteacher I teach a different subject each year. If there is no other positive outcome at least staff see that the head can get things wrong and have bad lessons. It permits the discussion of failure. I once organized, badly, a group of year-9 students to do a land-use survey along a local main road when I was teaching geography. Every outcome was achieved except the intellectual and the geographical. The students loved it, they were actively involved, paperwork was produced and I learnt a little about the teaching of geography and the organization of active learning!

Taking an example from the local further-education college, we have developed very successful sixth-form workshops in English, mathematics, science, arts and humanities. The whole of mathematics teaching is now done on a workshop basis using the Secondary Mathematics Independent Learning Experience (SMILE) system developed by the Inner London Education Authority. The essence of a workshop approach is that, as in a garage or in a tailor's, workers beaver away at individual or group tasks. In the best workshops the workers decide their own targets and set their own work schedules. There are supervisors, of course, who are available when things become tricky and who can help workers with their scheduling and target-setting. Of the available models of education I prefer that of student as co-worker in an educational enterprise. It places the teacher firmly in the role of manager. Models that assign the role of product or raw material to the student I find distressing.

The advent of computers aids this swing to student-led learning. In mathematics and English particularly, the use of computers is allowing more flexibility in the ways in which students use their time. Perversely, it is the scarcity of the machines that means the teacher cannot say, 'Now will you all . . .'.

The advent of local management of schools has allowed us to increase the capitation for each faculty by about 50 per cent. I hope that this will further assist the movement to active learning. I am conscious that in some small schools and in schools with falling rolls, formula funding does not permit capitation to be increased.

The new National Curriculum technology is also creating a revolution. I have known schools, even in the year of writing this chapter, in which teachers have said: 'I am a teacher of fabrics, I can't teach cookery'. Teachers with these same qualifications are now in Carlton-Bolling College teaching a generic technology course in which the student, or more usually groups of students, are directing their own learning. Their work encompasses home economics, craft design technology, business studies and information technology. This is a revolution, in our case decided upon by the teachers themselves in advance of the National Curriculum. The new performing-arts syllabus also encourages similar co-operative developments.

Another spur to the development of interesting styles of teaching and learning (interesting to the student, that is) was provided by our acceptance of the two-year framework of the Certificate of Pre-Vocational Education (CPVE). In this scheme all students are entered for CPVE and take part in the recording of achievement. They all have access to the 'enhancements' of that course and even 'straight A-level' students are now taking time in workshop activities to enhance their education.

The concept of 'enhancement' requires an understanding of the failure of the traditional sixth-form curriculum to provide an adequate diet for a growing teenager. Enhancements, ranging from 'business Spanish' to 'welding for beginners', encompass such courses as make the International Baccalaureate the varied diet some privileged youngsters enjoy. The idea of a two-year A-level course that lacks either work experience or community service, fortunately, now shares the fate of the dinosaurs: initially difficult to get rid of but not missed overmuch. Because students are making decisions about their own lives and the education therein, they take a more interested and more active role in the content of lessons. This is not always comfortable for the teacher, but then the oyster does not necessarily appreciate the piece of grit that produces the pearl.

More students than ever before are taking up the enterprise challenge in our college. In many different ways we are being successful in allowing students to achieve on their own initiative. It may be a trip to a theatre or a meal provided for some group of visitors. More formally, it may be a response to the Young Enterprise scheme, or a week spent at the nearby enterprise centre. Certainly all students now have two periods of work experience during their stay at the college, two weeks in year 10 and two weeks again in year 12. Our students come from an area where many people's experience of life suggests that, whatever they do, matters are bound to get worse. We aim to persuade students that they can achieve something by their own unaided effort or, more frequently, by the co-operative effort they make with others.

We take a staggered two-week holiday at what used to be Whit Week. Some staff take the two weeks finishing at the end of the Spring Bank Holiday week; others take a fortnight's holiday beginning one week later. The students take the first of these. This provides ideal quiet surroundings for the examinations that now occur in the week before Whit and a team of invigilators who can concentrate on the job. In the two weeks following the Spring Bank Holiday week, year-10 students go out on work experience and their tutors visit them, acquiring a wider understanding of local commercial activity and community organization. The examinations continue and are invigilated by a specialist team. The rest of the teachers (including the year-9 tutors) concentrate on year-9 students, providing a wide variety of experiential situations for them to explore.

This is for us the happiest and most productive time of the year, in which students grow and mature. They learn about their own capabilities and about the value of teamwork. No one wants to go back to ordinary lessons at the end of it. Perhaps this period of the year will begin to have its own insidious influence. After all, why chop up time into units as short as 90 minutes? It is a method of organization that prevents site visits almost entirely, and that disrupts any 'design-and-make' activity into potentially meaningless fragments.

Throughout the taught curriculum we find it necessary to support the teacher in the classroom with a second teacher on as many occasions as possible. The reason for this is the students' varying language capabilities. It is necessary to establish the reasons for the difficulties some of them face in the classroom before we can help them.

Many of our families do not use the written word as a means of communication: no books; no magazines; no being read to before going to sleep; no newspaper to find out what's on the television; and no use for written notes from school. The same people probably know a thousand stories, are able to speak several languages (including a smattering of English) and are surviving on less money per week than you or I would consider adequate. The children learn English at school and operate largely in English outside the home, but without the early experience of written communication they are disadvantaged in our educational system.

For the reasons outlined above there is often little encouragement for homework – perhaps because there is nowhere to do it. If the pupil and the parent share little language and if there is little family experience of

English schooling, there may be few conversations about schoolwork at home. The pupil may spend one, two or three hours each night at the mosque learning to repeat the Koran in Arabic, word for word. This activity also has messages for the pupil about the value of particular sorts of learning.

It is no wonder, then, if some Asian families view schools with suspicion: they are run by white people who do not speak the common language, who do not share their deep knowledge of Koranic teaching, who do not appreciate what the family understands as learning and who persist in using strange written characters as a means of communication. Worse than this, children learn to speak a different language and learn the ways of westerners – not all of which are liked by the family.

If expatriate Britons were offered such educational provision for their children they would rapidly make their own arrangements! However, although we allow Christian denominations to run their own schools at the expense of the State, such privileges are not extended to Muslims.

The desire of a minority of Muslim parents to send their children to Muslim schools is entirely understandable. It is similar to the desire satisfied among a similar minority of Roman Catholic and Anglican parents. The effects of allowing Muslim schools to have voluntary-aided status might allow families more coherence but it might also lead to greater segregation. My black friends point out to me that black people have given integration a fair chance and it has benefited them little. I feel this issue is an unsuitable one for white people to solve and that the black citizens of the country should be given the freedom to find the way forward.

What is remarkable is that 15 to 20 pupils so disadvantaged by our educational system leave us each year to go on to higher education and that many now have professional qualifications. There is little difference between the achievement of pupils from these backgrounds and that of others. One of the reasons for this is the programme of language support. Another is our refusal to confuse attainment with ability. This confusion commonly accounts for the use of streaming as an organizational tool in schools. Many students need support in the classroom. The curriculum must be accessible to the student. The student is not the problem: the curriculum is the problem. If the school cannot find a solution then it, too, is part of the problem.

We have teams of teachers who circulate between classes, helping teachers to prepare materials that are accessible and who help students to have access to them. There are different threshold levels of English capability. For instance, a pupil straight off an aeroplane from the Indian sub-continent needs a certain level of language in order to understand classroom instructions and the menu at lunch. A higher level is needed when it comes to creating written work for GCSE English, and different skills are needed in order to reach, say, attainment target 7 in geography. 'Language support' needs to continue into the upper college for A-level study and for vocational units as specialist vocabulary and research techniques are required.

We take it for granted that students will achieve more in English if they are able to explore the written forms and the grammar of the language their parents speak. We also hope that the community will perceive the college as being more of an educational institution that supports the community if Asian languages are taught there. This means that where two or three languages would normally be an adequate offering, six are actually offered. The 'inefficiency' this creates in staffing the curriculum has been recognized until recently by section-11 grants from the Home Office. Urdu has been our main 'foreign' language and has provided valued experiences for over half of each cohort for several years now.

RELATIONSHIPS

The foundation of our policy on relationships in the college is that people work better and are more productive when they are trusted and when they are given responsibility and some control over their lives.

When the draft circular on the length of the school day came out it had an appendix that showed for a number of schools the length of time 'left over' at the end of 1,265 hours – a figure, I am glad to say, that is fading from teachers' minds. On the scale the circular used we had twice as much time 'left over' for professional discretion as the most 'lenient' school in the table. This has been deliberate: we need the average teacher to work long hours (I wish we could be less demanding) in order to run the college effectively. The people who choose to become teachers seem to be willing to sacrifice their lives to secure a decent deal for their charges. They are more likely to feel happy and fulfilled about it if this is clearly their decision.

This is, to my mind, what makes teaching a profession – its members are not 'hourly' inclined. The treatment of fellow teachers as professionals is not easy when there is such limited funding of education. I shadowed an industrial manager during an interview recently in which a local firm was hoping to select graduate trainees. This is equivalent to selecting graduates for a PGCE course. It was a two-day exercise and cost about £8,000 – an interesting comparison with the selection for PGCE.

I used to work for ICI where far more money is spent on capital projects than on salaries. The result of that is a freedom to spend perhaps as much again on each professional as his or her salary because it is still a small fraction of total investment. This means, for instance, first-class rail-fare and a three-star hotel when officers have to go away from home, whereas teachers can expect to pay for their own travel, take sandwiches and attend in-service training on Saturdays.

If we were to be able to treat teachers properly, the budget at Carlton-Bolling College (which at the time of writing was £1.5 million for teachers' salaries and £400,000 for everything else) should be increased to at least £3 million. The public has not yet been educated by the politicians (whose eyes should see far into the future) to accept the taxation levels that would enable teaching to compete adequately for the country's top brains.

Within the constraints of finance it is necessary to treat staff as valued investments. Some effort has gone into this and we enjoy very good re-lationships and a co-operative working atmosphere as staff ignore the ac-cumulated insults the underfunded system heaps on them. I look forward to appraisal to improve this atmosphere and to allow teachers to ask for – and to get – the resources they need to do the job. At the time of writing it is not clear whether a national system of appraisal will be developed, although there is a mood to increase spending on education among a wider group of the electorate. Political decisions will have to be taken whether to fund education properly or to allow the slide towards mediocrity to accelerate.

Over the past two years, particularly, I have been at pains to discover how people in the college feel about various issues. One outcome of this has been the development of student councils and staff quality circles. Student councils are not new and we have perhaps been slow to develop them. Their formation has had a beneficial influence on the political aware-ness of students and on their confidence to speak out. The rules we have adopted are simple: if they have anything to say to me they first send their elected representatives to disuss this with me and then they put their com-plaints or suggestions in writing. I promise to reply in writing and have provided noticeboards so that the letters can be displayed side by side. Issues so far have included the following:

● Request for a year-11 common room (granted).
● Criticisms about toilets (acknowledged as valid, changes made).
● Requests to modify uniform (some modification allowed).
● Requests for lockers (furniture money diverted to buy more).
● Application for noticeboard space (granted).
● Request for ties to be optional (refused).

I am keen to maintain student interest in the councils and therefore have an interest in satisfying their requests or giving good reason, which they accept, for not doing so. If ever they felt ignored they would consider the council as pointless. My second aim, only now being realized, is to provide the councils with income about which they have to make spending decisions. We are achieving this by giving them lockers to rent out to the members of their year group. They keep the rental and make decisions about the way in which it is spent.

Staff quality circles are voluntary groups that take responsibility for continuously reviewing an aspect of the college: for instance, one focuses on residentials, while another considers health and safety. Even in their early days there have been noticeable changes in the 'ownership' of college life among members of the circles.

Relationships with parents pose particular challenges because of the predominant 'whiteness' of the teaching staff and the high numbers of students who have parents born in the Indian sub-continent. Smith and Tomlinson remark on how difficult it is for such parents to get into white schools.[1] The combination of uncertainty in the language of communication and the traditional respect for the profession make for reticent parents who, nevertheless, are very concerned for their child's progress into adulthood. As one parent-governor said to me, 'My father took me to school and said to me "This teacher is now also your father" and he said to the teacher "Here is your son".'

Our college has just won a trophy for the school in England and Wales that has the best communication with parents. I have to say that the judges considered only the written evidence we presented and did not consider our success in attracting our parents into the college.

Parents will come into the college when the purpose is to consult about the progress of their children but not for other purposes. Our parent–teacher organization closed down some years ago when, of the eight parents at the annual general meeting, none wished to take office. It is frustrating to know that parents in general are so desperately concerned about the way in which their offspring are growing up, yet so unable to work with the college as partners in many of the ways that would help their children.

We are successful in attracting adults (mainly white) into the college for the purposes of studying. We offer a free crèche and free tuition in upper-college (sixth-form) classes. We also offer space to community groups during the day and enjoy, for instance, the presence of a crown-green bowling club in the winter when their greens are too wet to bowl on. The pensioners are a bit rowdy but are full of fun and add to the village atmosphere.

In the early part of the 1989–90 college year, we seconded one of the deputies at our own cost to develop links with local industry and commerce. The venture was very successful and I would recommend the idea to any school seeking to widen the opportunities for its students. Although money was forthcoming the main benefit was the closer relationships with the world 'out there'.

Governors are important to any institution. At Carlton-Bolling College they must bridge the cultural divide between a largely white staff and mainly Asian parents. Governors need to be aware of committee structure and procedure. What are minutes for? What does the chairperson do in a discussion? People with this sort of expertise do not generally choose to live in the inner city. Those who do live there find themselves spread rather thinly across many good causes. Carlton-Bolling has, at the time of writing, just lost its fifth chair of governors in five years. The lure of power in the Education Reform Act 1988 does not seem to attract many parents to serve in our area.

PERSONAL REFLECTIONS

The first thing that strikes me about headship is a confirmation of Charles Handy's conclusion that schools have insufficient time in which to manage.[2] There are so many proper management tools I and other of the senior staff should be using in review, evaluation, training, monitoring and in other fields that we simply do not have time to use. This provokes shameful feelings of hostility towards inspectors and advisers who themselves are under equally difficult constraints, but who find time to make us feel guilty about forms unfilled and procedures unfollowed. This was the situation even before the head took responsibility for asbestos and windows!

I have felt for many years that, after the sheltered period of probation, teaching is done in a teacher's spare time. The task is approached with a part of the teacher's mind that functions automatically as other issues claim the conscious area of the brain. There is great conflict between the important and the urgent. For the head, and for other staff who have their sights set on management of units larger than the classroom, the problem is worse than for the teacher who is content to teach.

Speaking of upward mobility, heads experience a difficulty of which any classteacher reading this account may be unaware. After changing jobs and moving house every four or five years in pursuit of promotion, the situation of *being* a head and having *no prospects* requires a totally new mental set. Every change of job thereafter the head might contemplate involves more committee and office work and perhaps a drop in pay – certainly less direct influence on the education of young people. The alternative, for someone appointed at the age of, say, 40 years to a headship after a nomadic teaching career of eighteen years, is another twenty years in the same job and the same school.

I think this is a powerful argument for short-term contracts for heads and for a pay structure that encourages people to take a second headship. If you *have* to move to a new job and area and it isn't perfect . . . well, that's life, isn't it? If you choose to move because you are just afraid of going stale, and it costs you money to move, and you don't get a pay rise, *and* it isn't perfect . . . well, that is your own silly fault, as your family will no doubt remark.

A head wears comfortable grooves in the job and surrounds the office with congenial people over a period of years. A head forgets the wretched tiredness of the last period on Friday and the 35th report in the desperation of midnight. Worse still, there grows some degree of respect in the neighbourhood for this person with an aura of power. Schools actually benefit from the nervous energy of the insecurity of a head's first few years and suffer from the contentment induced by comfort. I am thinking of buying a hair shirt, it will be cheaper than moving.

There is a danger for the headteacher of a large school of being isolated in an office dealing with a telephone and with paperwork. If the college had more senior staff I would get rid of the head's office altogether. All the paperwork would be done more efficiently by others who could brief me on what I really needed to know. The obsession with paper communication would go and I would get rid of all my pens, the computer and the paper-clips. I should then walk the corridors, *talk* with students and with staff, visit lessons and know the college in a way that is now only achieved in casual moments.

It is highly likely that the head forms judgements about staff in a large school on the basis of very little data, and it is by no means certain that appraisal will change this. An analysis of the data-gathering conversations a headteacher has during a week would show that some people figured more largely than others. Among the most frequent would possibly be the deputies, but also an assortment of staff selected purely on the basis that they want and feel able to talk to the head.

The head who decides to speak with a more representative selection of people each week has to engineer conversations with reticent staff and deny conversation with more voluble staff. This conflicts with the principle that the head should be available to those of the staff who feel a need to talk.

Every conversation is of great importance and will be remembered by the other party when it has been forgotten by the head. The ill-advised speculation drawn out by the apparently disinterested colleague will be produced in evidence, possibly by someone completely different, at a later but more relevant time. This phenomenon has the effect of making the head a distant and unapproachable person who measures his or her words in a manner that could be described by the unkind as pompous. It further distances the head from the teaching force. The restricted nature of the head's data-base means that the opinions of the close, trusted advisers assumes great importance. *Even though it is likely to be biased* by the perceptions and desires of the adviser, the head may welcome it as impartial opinion and may have no recent relevant experience against which to triangulate it.

My solution to the problem has been to obtain a pedometer that measures how far I walk in a day at the college. On a good day I can do 10 miles, but there are depressing days when 1½ by lunchtime becomes 1¾ by 4.30 p.m. Management by walking about is a well-respected technique and I have adopted 'distance travelled' as a personal performance indicator. The more people I meet in a day, people who have not sought me out, the wider the base of opinion I have against which to judge advice.

I should like to see many changes in education. I should like to see smaller schools with a wider age range and with less dependence upon a timetable. The time teachers and students spend together determines the quality of the relationship and of the learning. Schools with a maximum of 500 students and with a lively community involvement, using time in blocks of one day or so with teachers working in teams to present the National Curriculum would be better places in which to learn. Studies in the USA indicate a much higher level of participation among students in small schools than in large ones. The argument about increased opportunities in large schools does not hold water.

The 'general public' must be led to realize that the purchasing power of their pensions will be determined by the quality of the education of the young people now in schools, even the poor ones from the inner city. This is all the more urgent because increasing numbers of taxpayers do not have children in school and are more interested in the provision of homes for the elderly than they are in the education service. Who will be the first major politician to take up this challenge?

The differential funding required to provide education for a child from a low-income inner-city or rural home, compared with a child from the affluent suburbs from where most of the taxes are collected, has been ignored. This is especially the case in those same suburbs where it is easy to think that the poor have had no hand in generating the wealth that justifies the taxes!

The funds necessary to provide visits, residentials, music, fieldwork and a host of other experiences I provide for my own children out of school, together with the extra school hours to provide these, cannot be found by reducing the funding to suburban schools. We need extra, new money and it is in all our interests that it should be found.

Being a headteacher is a great job and will become better as local management takes hold. The ability to deploy resources to produce the most effective educational provision is an exciting one. Many of us were not selected for this entrepreneurial streak and find it stressful, but I enjoy it.

The real joy in upper schools is to see pupils become adults, to see pupils from educationally disadvantaged backgrounds become confident and competent. It is particularly encouraging to see confident girls leaving school who will not instantly be looking for a man to lean on but who will develop into interesting people in their own right. It is not necessary for such people to come back to say 'thank you', although we would hope that we had also imparted the basics of courtesy. The reward is in the irreversible change from powerless to powerful.

Commentary

Flecknoe values the nature of the traditional village environment where relationships with respected elders and peers were pivotal to the learning process. He also believes that school administrative systems should be simple. This maxim has led him to develop a three-period timetable and a lean senior-management structure. The longer, fewer periods are designed to encourage time for good working relationships to be forged between teachers and students and for active learning strategies to be developed.

The issue of students taking an active role in, and responsibility for, their learning has already been commented on by Collings (Chapter 2) and will be referred to in subsequent chapters: for Flecknoe it is very important. This attitude towards pupils has not always been encouraged by headteachers, and schools have been criticized for producing pupils who are passive, over-dependent learners. In contrast, those who have been encouraged to think for themselves – even though they may, at times, be more challenging to teach – should be better equipped to cope with life after school.

Like other contributors leading inner-city schools, Flecknoe is aware of the day-to-day achievements of many families living in very disadvantaged circumstances. He recognizes, too, the additional educational hurdles facing some members of the Asian community, such as the lack of a shared common language and the necessity of regular attendance at Koranic classes. He is alone, however, in questioning whether or not Muslim families should be able to send their children to Muslim schools, with voluntary-aided status. Though sympathetic to their desires, Flecknoe concedes that 'the issue is an unsuitable one for white people to solve'.

Like Alston (Chapter 1), Flecknoe is concerned about the lack of incentives and opportunities for career progression for established headteachers. He suggests short-term contracts and pay incentives. Other educational appointments are beginning to reflect these practices.

REFERENCES

1. Smith, D. J. and Tomlinson, S. (1989) *The School Effect: A Study of Multiracial Comprehensives*, Policy Studies Institute, London.
2. Handy, C. (1984) *Taken for Granted? Understanding Schools as Organisations*, Longman, Harlow, Essex.

4
Vasanthi Rao
Handsworth Wood Girls School

Vasanthi Rao obtained a BA and a BEd from the University of Madras.
After teaching for ten years in India she came to Britain where, for a while,
she worked in a factory. She returned to teaching in 1969. From 1982 she was
headteacher of Handsworth Wood Girls School in Birmingham. She has
recently retired.

I arrived in Birmingham in May 1967 with my family, with a teaching
voucher and a head full of dreams. Having only £2.50 in my pocket was no
problem because I thought there would be a job waiting for me. Alas, the
truth was very different! When I contacted the LEA, I was told that those
who had qualifications from abroad needed to obtain Qualified Teacher
Status (QTS) from the DES. So the battle began. Applications and copies
of degree certificates went forward and back to the DES and LEA. After
six months, provisional QTS was granted, with the condition that I obtain a
post within a specified period. So now it was up to the LEA. Every application I made brought the same reply: 'No vacancy at present'. This state of
affairs was very difficult to understand.

I was a graduate from Madras University with mathematics as a main,
and science as a subsidiary subject. I had ten years teaching experience in
large mixed secondary schools. There was a shortage of mathematics
teachers and I had been given the entry permit to the UK with a voucher.
But no teaching post transpired!

Meanwhile, my husband, daughter and myself had to eat, have a roof
over our heads and prepare for winter. I was getting desperate, in a foreign
country without any family or friends – I had to get a job. I started looking

for any other opening. I approached an agency and also started looking in local papers. I went round offices and firms looking for a vacancy. But a trained teacher, not equipped with any other skills, such as typing, was not in demand. Fortunately there was a laboratory technician job available in a plastics firm. When I was offered that job it was like reaching heaven. The problem was solved temporarily. I worked at that factory for twenty months. I must admit that it was the best and most useful experience I ever had. Working with 18–20-year-olds (I was 30 at that time) helped me to understand the western way of life, learn the colloquial language and build my confidence. The two supervisors who got to know me urged me to persevere to get into teaching. With their help and my effort, at last I was called for an interview. That was a daunting experience, with a panel of eight people interviewing me in the Council House. I must have convinced them because they offered me a job on a six-weeks trial period and made it clear that I was taking the risk of losing my job if I did not succeed. But I had confidence in my teaching ability.

I went to a girls school. Mine was the only coloured face among staff and students. I was covering a maternity leave. It was hard (not the teaching of my subject, but managing a group of teenage girls from working-class backgrounds). The last thing they wanted to learn was mathematics. I must confess I was insecure and very vulnerable, not knowing whom to approach for help and support. I managed to keep my head above water and survived the six weeks. Then I had to do two years' probation and it felt as if I were on trial for ever. But my commitment to teaching, my past experience and, most of all, my need to survive in a foreign land, made me persevere and I was on my way!

After teaching in the first school for four years (I was given a scale-2 allowance after two years), I was appointed head of mathematics in another girls school. This was a school on the threshold of new developments. The newly appointed headteacher was bringing in positive changes, raising standards as well as the ethos of the school. Changes were necessary because of the Raising of the School Leaving Age (ROSLA). There had to be relevant courses. Along with CSE and O-level courses, we developed courses for leisure and a number of mode-3 examination courses. As part of the leisure courses I tried Indian cookery, costumes and arts. All the girls from year 5 and also some members of staff took part. This was fun and enjoyed by all. Mode-3 courses were more difficult to establish. They needed a great deal of preparation by teachers and coursework from pupils, but this gave me an opportunity to meet teachers from other schools and to widen my experience. Girls benefited by achieving good grades in their CSE examinations. The headteacher backed me in every way, giving moral and financial support. When one starts in a new school, trying to bring in changes, it is important to have the wholehearted support from the top and I was fortunate in this.

There was also change in the population of the school with more Asian girls coming into it. This was the opportunity I was waiting for. I had enough experience, enthusiasm, commitment and the support of a good headteacher. I developed the mathematics department using new materials and teaching techniques and motivated the girls to do well. I worked with my other colleagues and established many extra-curricular activities.

Those were the days when multicultural education was introduced and considered to be an important issue. It was important in this school because we had to raise the awareness of the staff to the needs of the girls and also teach all pupils about the background and culture of others so that they understood and respected each other. The curriculum had to be developed, the language issues to be tackled and the parents educated. Again, it was hard work but rewarding and satisfying.

After three years as head of department, I was fortunate to be appointed as deputy head at the same school. People think that internal promotion is not a good idea, but at this school it worked for me. I was able to maintain the continuity, knowing every girl and most of the parents. So I was able to carry on with the developmental work. It was not easy because there were two other colleagues who had been interviewed for the post and I had to work with them. There were others who had been in that school longer than me who felt a little jealous and there were some obstacles. But the majority of the staff were with me. I must confess these were the best and most enjoyable years of my career.

When the headteacher left to take up the headship of a larger school, I was in charge of the school for a term. I wanted to carry on, but a new head was appointed. It was difficult to get used to the new head. I was very attached to the pupils and parents and it was difficult to let go. The new head wanted changes and, like everyone, I wanted to resist these. I felt I knew the pupils and their needs. But, looking back, I realize we are in schools for the benefit of the pupils, not to boost our own ego.

The next three years were totally different. I got a thorough grounding to face the new challenges and changes that were taking place in education, such as governing bodies, equal opportunities, and so on. I was encouraged to go on management courses, implement change in school, chair various committees and represent the school at meetings. It took some time to get used to the new regime but, looking back, it was all worth it.

THE SCHOOL

I was appointed headteacher of my present school in 1982. It is a four-form entry school, with 650 girls in the 11–19 age-group. The majority of girls are from an Asian background, with a few Afro-Caribbeans and very few whites. There are forty members of staff and seven non-teaching staff.

The school is situated in a lovely part of the inner city, with a tree-lined frontage and grass and flower beds. The building is 33 years old, a typical 1950s structure. There is also a boys school on the same campus and we share a middle building with them. You can imagine the problems we face: two single-sex schools sharing a campus and also a building. Since 1983 we have also run a combined sixth form.

Boys and girls come from the same area – they are related, neighbours or friends. They meet and talk to each other in the house, in the Gurdwaras and at family functions. But when they reach the school campus we segregate them, to the extent that they cannot look at each other or talk to each other. It is an artificial barrier we create. In a way I blame the parents for imposing these restrictions; the community for exaggerating innocent meetings. This will make the youngsters go behind our backs to meet their friends. Of course, a girls' school, especially a school with a majority of Asian girls, attracts boys and men like bees round a honeypot.

The majority of the girls come from deprived families, and the school is eligible for a social-priority allowance. It has very high standards, both academic and social. Examination results are good compared to other schools in the area (most of them above the national average), there is good discipline and all girls wear school uniform. There is always demand for places and, to date, the school has no declining-roll problem.

We receive pupils from 25 to 35 primary schools (this has increased because of parental choice). We maintain good links with our main feeder schools so that there is continuity for our pupils. The ability of the pupils is very varied. There are severe problems with language, as English is the second language for a majority of the pupils. Most of our girls speak Punjabi, Urdu, Bengali or Vietnamese at home. They are bilingual, in some cases multilingual. Their parents may not speak English. As a result they enter infant school at a disadvantage. There are not enough bilingual teachers or classroom assistants to help these children. They go through primary education without reaching the standards they are capable of and are not able to catch up in secondary school. The National Curriculum, I hope, will help to overcome this, especially if testing is carried out using bilingual techniques, or even in the pupils' home language.

PERSONAL PHILOSOPHY OF EDUCATION

When I was appointed as head of this school, I was asked what was my aim. My answer was the same as any other head I guess: 'All-round education for all the pupils'. The majority of them being Asian girls did not make any difference: we live in a multi-ethnic society and we hope our school will reflect in its work the richness and diversity of many cultures and will cater consistently and sympathetically for the many and various needs of our pupils. We aim to provide for the basic needs of individual pupils in literacy and numeracy and to create and sustain a stimulating atmosphere whereby pupils will be able to fulfil their potential. We hope to develop in our pupils confidence, judgement and self-discipline and also to encourage in them the means by which they can form satisfactory personal relationships.

By the end of their school life, we hope that each girl will have developed the ability to make informed choices and be able to take her place with confidence in a rapidly changing society.

ORGANIZATION OF LEARNING

We try to implement these aims by adopting an appropriate curriculum. We use relevant teaching methods and provide a relaxed but structured framework within which pupils can obtain the maximum – academically and socially. Improving standards and achieving good results are always at the top of our priorities. We start from where our girls are – their ability, their language, their home background, and so on. We respect the very rich culture they bring into school. We respect their religion and tradition. We work with parents and community to give the best to our girls.

We consider the school has to help to bridge the gap between home and the outside world. Most of our parents come from the villages in Punjab, Pakistan or Bangladesh, mostly from farming backgrounds. Some of them have not experienced school life. They may be illiterate in their own languages. They have not all moved with the times. Many are still thinking of their village life and the restrictions they had when they were young. They have lost touch with their own country and with how it has developed. They live among their own community so they do not come into contact with the outside world. Because of the lack of language they cannot understand what is going on. They live in perpetual fear of the evils of society, dishonour of the family and losing respect in the community. They are guided by community or religious leaders who may be after personal glory.

Parents under the influence of these people impose restrictions on their children – especially the girls.

The youngsters born and brought up here have a different outlook. They are influenced by their white peers and the media. They go out, in a limited way, enough to make them realize the difference between their family way of life and life outside. They crave for the freedom they lack, but sometimes when given it, do not know how to use it.

THE EDUCATION OF ASIAN GIRLS

Let me concentrate on the education of Asian girls. In school, we try to create an atmosphere where they can relate to their home culture and to Western culture. Our curriculum is multicultural, anti-racist and anti-sexist. We encourage bilingualism and community languages. We learn about the religions of the world and visit places of worship. We encourage girls to learn about each other's food and clothes. This does not mean we go completely one way. As I said, 'Educating the whole child' is our aim, so we make sure our curriculum meets the requirements of examination standards. Language development is one of our priorities and we have managed to achieve very high results in English language, well above the national average. Our girls achieve their grades in French, as well as in Punjabi, Urdu or Bengali.

Equal opportunities is uppermost in our minds – gender and race. We encourage girls to go into further and higher education. We expose them to careers that were considered to be male orientated. Technology plays a very important role in the curriculum. We are one of the few girls schools with a well-equipped craft, design and technology suite where girls can experience the new technology. Computers are used across the curriculum.

Appropriate careers guidance is given from the early stages in year 9. Girls are made aware of the opportunities available to them. Every girl goes on a fortnight's work experience in years 10–11, to make her aware of what the world of work is like and what will be expected of her. Visits are arranged for girls to see various fields of work. Visiting speakers are invited into school to give information about various careers and also to provide an opportunity for students to meet outsiders. Members of staff are encouraged to go on industrial placements so that they are made aware of the changing needs of industry in order to equip the pupils accordingly. The Industrial Society has played a very useful role in this area by organizing conventions in school and courses for staff.

By providing a suitable curriculum and training and by creating opportunities for pupils to develop, we hope to achieve all our aims. This is a challenging task. When students leave our school, approximately 70 per cent of them remain in full-time education, in sixth forms in schools or colleges. They follow A-level or BTEC courses. Some retake GCSEs to try to improve their grades. About 14 per cent go on to training schemes and about 8 per cent enter employment – mainly banking, building societies or the Civil Service. The rest either work in the family business or stay at home. About 8 per cent are unemployed.

From our own sixth form, 5 per cent go into higher education (polytechnic or universities) often to read business studies, law or sciences. Our higher-achieving girls tend to go to colleges to do their A-levels and we lose contact with, and also credit for, them. These girls feel they need a change from school. They consider there is more freedom in colleges. Added to this is the attraction of travelling out of the area where they live and away from its peer pressures. Undoubtedly there is also an element of 'the grass is greener' in their decision.

The majority of parents support our efforts to educate their girls to go into further education, except for a few Muslim parents who feel education is not important, as their daughters will be married off. Unfortunately for them, many boys want girls with good qualifications, so parents are having to change their views. Changing attitudes is one of the most difficult things. Girls who are brought up to listen and to obey at home have to be trained to think for themselves, make decisions and take initiatives. Their confidence has to be built up and opportunities given to practise exercising it. Drama plays a vital role in this. Also important is the school council where representatives of the class meet an appointed member of staff in order to discuss issues related to the running of the school and to make decisions. The prefect system in year 11 gives pupils the opportunities to take responsibility and to carry out their duties, as a responsible person is expected to do.

The Personal and Social Education (PSE) programme in the school also contributes towards this. From year 7 to 13 there is a continuous programme that brings in relationships, responsibilities (to self and others), decision-making, health education, careers education and social and moral issues.

Study skills are very important, more so than ever now, because of the principles of GCSE. Coursework plays an important role in the final grades and pupils have to realize that they need to work continuously and meet the set targets regarding their assessments, essays and projects. They have to do a great deal of research and learn to put it together. The old method of attending lessons in the class, revising near the examination and writing for two to three hours at a time is gone. It takes time for pupils to get used to this idea, especially Asian pupils and parents for whom the emphasis has been always on the written examination. For them, if one does not produce pages and pages of notes in the classroom, it is not a good lesson: if there is no written examination at the end, it is not a good course. So new teaching techniques and student-centred learning are contrary to their expectations. If Asian parents observe a lesson where there is group or discussion work going on and see the 'organized chaos', they raise their hands in horror. For them, a good lesson is pupils sitting quietly and listening to the teacher and copying notes from the blackboard or from dictation.

Parents, however, do want a good education for their daughters. They are very ambitious in their hopes. They expect high grades in examinations. When it is time to select subject options, they want their daughters to take the three sciences. When they come to parents' evenings, they are happy to talk to English, mathematics and science teachers. In the Asian tradition, these subjects have a high profile. The Indian education system is very commendable but it defeats the objective of the school – 'Education of the whole child' – developing all-round skills pupils need to lead a successful life as an adult. It is not possible for everyone to become a doctor or an engineer or a computer programmer. There are other worthwhile careers – teaching, nursing, the police, and so on. One has to consider the ability and aptitude of the students. Does anyone ask them what they want? Or do parents decide they know it all? I believe there should be proper guidance, consultation and, of course, high expectations from everyone, pupil, parent and teachers.

What about the teachers? Changing attitudes is as difficult here, perhaps more so. Teachers are very much creatures of habit and they do not like changes. For many of them the old didactic teaching method has brought good results and has helped to maintain so-called 'good standards and discipline'. Yes, students went into further and higher education, but how many? Most probably the pupils were taught in streamed groups, and the top 20 per cent succeeded, while the rest had an education totally irrelevant to them. This demotivated them and they went through an education system without gaining academic or social skills. Of course, in earlier days there was plenty of employment and people fitted in. Perhaps people were satisfied and content with less and there were not many temptations.

Times have changed. Now the needs are different. People are ambitious, they want more. They know their rights. The skills needed for employment are different. The so-called shop-floor work that was hard and dirty is getting more and more technical, skilled and clean. That is why we, in school, have to train our pupils to be receptive to new ideas and help them to acquire the necessary skills.

Our duty is to *all* pupils – not just the top 20 per cent. That means we have to provide a relevant and interesting curriculum for all. We have to provide for the needs of the pupils and help them to overcome their difficulties in learning our language. This can be done through a structured academic and pastoral programme.

MANAGEMENT OF THE SCHOOL

I inherited a school where there were high standards, both academic and disciplinary. Staff and students were told what to do and they did it. Everything looked well on the surface and gave a good impression. But when I looked at the curriculum provided and the organization, I was not happy. I felt every pupil was not receiving her entitlement. I wanted to build on the experience of the girls and their rich culture and tradition and, at the same time, train them to meet the needs of a fast-changing society.

I tried the banding system – top, middle and bottom bands. This, I hoped, would meet the needs of all by stretching the more able at the top, moving at a slower pace in the middle and providing extra support at the bottom. Every pupil was given the same opportunity and facility. The schemes of work were modified to make them relevant and interesting. Suitable vocational courses were introduced through business education, food and nutrition and child development. My regret was that I was not able to provide technical and craft (so-called 'boys' crafts') courses because of a lack of facilities. I tried sending the girls to a neighbouring craft centre, which was a great success but it did not cater for all. The constant battle and perseverance did bring results and we now have full facilities.

Health education played an important role: healthy eating, personal hygiene, the dangers of smoking and of drugs. In the past four years we have organized sessions to give information on AIDS to girls in year 11. We made use of outside agencies: the health authority, police, voluntary organizations and also the packages produced by the DES, the media and other organizations and publishers. We have provided opportunities for interaction between pupils and pupils; pupils and teachers; and pupils and outside speakers. This has created an openness and removed certain myths associated with drugs, AIDS, etc.

A sex-education policy was drafted, though sex education was already taking place in school through biology, health-education and child-development courses. We formalized the policy after discussions with staff and parents. We had to be sensitive to certain issues, so as not to offend parents. We always made sure parents were aware of what we were doing, who was leading the sessions and what was the content. Parents were always welcome to come to discuss these issues if they were concerned, and to withdraw their daughters from certain sessions. We had one or two who objected to a detailed programme of sex education. Some of them allowed their daughters to listen and take part in discussions up to a certain level, but write nothing. Only one parent refused and the girl had to be withdrawn.

In my 21 years of teaching in the UK, a full HMI visit never took place in the schools where I was teaching but we had many day visits, subject reviews and surveys conducted in schools. Being a single-sex school, in an inner-city area with pupils from minority groups, this was inevitable. The reports we received were mostly very encouraging, with helpful criticism regarding allocation of scarce resources or the adaptation of suitable teaching methods in certain areas. As a result of these visits, I came to know many of the HMIs and was invited to take part in national and international conferences and to sit on certain committees. These were very rewarding experiences, and I will discuss them later.

We had many LEA reviews, again in specific subjects where results have been particularly good or bad. The English department was in the 'good' category. The literature used was varied, from Shakespeare, Thomas Hardy and Charles Dickens to Faroukh Dhondy, Rosa Guy and Ruksana Smith. Despite difficulties over staff continuity (teachers leaving for promotion or to have a baby) and the different teaching methods (from very traditional to very modern), the results were consistently good. Considering the girls' background, the results were really outstanding. On average, about 20 per cent take GCSE English early, in year 10, and pass. Of those who take it in year 11, about 90 per cent gain a grade C or above. Almost everyone gains a pass grade in English language, despite the fact that about a third of the pupils enter the school with a reading age below their chronological age.

As I said before, development of language was our priority. The special-needs department worked hard in this area in the lower years, using practical and bilingual approaches. Staff motivate the pupils by taking them on visits, giving extra help in reading clubs and encouraging them to use appropriate language wherever they could. Support from English as a second language teachers has been invaluable in this area. This language development, I hope, helped the pupils to achieve higher grades in other subject areas. The results have been good, considering the ability of the girls who come into the school at the age of 11.

One of the criticisms that came out was how we labelled some girls as the 'bottom group'. We did not call it the bottom group or special-needs group but the girls themselves worked it out. The attitude of some staff did not help. We used to go by primary-school records, the comments we received from the teachers and the 'tests' conducted in the first half-term of the first year of secondary school. We knew these tests were not accurate and they were culture-biased with language and content not suitable for our types of pupils. But they provided some initial guide. We knew it was unfair to judge pupils on the basis of these tests. We monitored their progress carefully and there was always room for movement. But it was not entirely satisfactory.

After much discussion, consultation and weighing of all the pros and cons, we started to teach in mixed-ability groups. We have tried to keep the group size to about 24. This is costly on staffing but beneficial to the pupils. There has been a considerable amount of in-service, both internal and external, for the teachers. It would be ideal if we could have more collaborative teaching involving the special-needs department, but Birmingham LEA staffing ratio does not allow for this. We hope that, under local management of schools (LMS), we may be able to do something about it.

Mixed ability teaching is not easy. It is more difficult in certain subjects than others. Teachers have to work hard to prepare suitable materials and to change their teaching methods. We are hoping to convert some by showing them good practice, through discussions with those who have succeeded, and by giving extra support in the class. But I am not sure we will succeed with everyone. All the in-service, resources and material will not change all attitudes. Have we heard this before?

The Education Reform Act 1988, in a way, has helped us to achieve our aims regarding all pupils reaching certain standards at certain levels. The Technical and Vocational Education Initiative (TVEI) will back it up by emphasizing the entitlement of all pupils in technology, science, work experience and records of achievement. At our school we are already on the way; it only needs firming up in certain aspects. We have been providing the core subjects specified in the National Curriculum for many years. There may be some problems in convincing parents regarding balanced science (two options) instead of three sciences. But, again, that is coping with the change – fear or suspicion of anything new. Regarding the foundation subjects, there is no problem in years 7, 8 and 9. But if required to do all seven subjects to specific attainment levels, or GCSE equivalent, we may face certain problems regarding the ability of all pupils doing up to ten subjects and the time factor – how can you fit in all subjects in 25 hours teaching time per week? We have to wait and see. With so many uncertainties, disagreements and consultation documents, things may change. We can only do the groundwork and prepare a framework at this time.

We have had both useful and highly emotional discussions regarding the modern-language issue. The languages being promoted by the DES meet the European needs of 1992, but what about pupil entitlement and equal opportunities for pupils from minority groups? What about community languages? Should some of them not be included as modern languages? (Then came a revised regulation, which included some community languages.) How should we interpret the Act? It says languages have to be offered. Not every pupil, however, has to do them. In our school we always encourage every girl to learn at least one language, either French or their own language. In some cases girls do French *and* their own language. Now we hope to provide French and one of the community languages so that we can meet the needs of 1992 as well as the needs at home. The major problem we face, like many other schools, is finding modern-language teachers.

The place of religious education and collective worship in the school are other interesting issues. Again, we have offered religious education as one of the examination subjects for many years. It is very popular because of the nature of the syllabus. Some parents have attended assemblies and discussed what we do. They are satisfied with our practice. No one has yet asked to hold their own act of worship. We also tackle the social and moral issues in PSE lessons and in a life-skills course in years 10 and 11.

Collective worship? Well, in a school like ours, we had stopped holding Christian assemblies many years ago. We always adopt a moral theme, common to all religions. We talk about, and give information about, religions and we invite religious/community leaders to take part in the assemblies. We encourage girls to talk about their religions and how they celebrate their festivals. This is education, a sharing of experience, and this is what we should do in school. It is not our place to preach, especially when there are so many religions represented in school and also people who are atheist and humanitarian. We have assemblies that are suitable to all, we pray to our own gods, we talk about and practise (I hope) what we learn. I hope we meet the requirements of the Act by adapting the moral issues that are Christian but also common to other religions. I do not believe in segregating pupils to have special assemblies, conducted by individual religious leaders. It is not physically possible nor practical. In our school, at present, there are no withdrawals from assembly (staff or pupils), except Jehovah's Witnesses.

Aspects of the National Curriculum I applaud are the cross-curricular issues, such as environment, economic awareness, etc. Again, we have been trying, for many years, to break down subject barriers and to encourage people to share their areas of experience. Teachers are very protective and defensive about their subjects and resources, rarely sharing. It is 'my subject, my room or my equipment'. As a result, student learning is compartmentalized. The graphs they learn in mathematics are not applied to geography, nor is the function of nutrients learnt in science related to the food they cook in home economics. As a result, there is much repetition and waste of time and resources!

If the National Curriculum specifies that all subjects have to be taught up to certain levels, it can be done only by some aspects of subjects being dealt with in a cross-curricular way and the rest in a specialist way. This will be another change we have to manage. Given the time and resources, I am sure teachers will do it. We have already found it happening in Technical and Vocational Education (TVE) where funds are made available for resources especially in science and technology areas: support staff (teaching and non-teaching) are provided for developing careers education and vocational courses; and funds are available for staff training and for teachers working in their own time after school hours. This has given some incentive to teachers, not just financial but also a recognition of what they are doing and the opportunity to share ideas and experiences with colleagues from other institutions in the partnership. Having a good co-ordinator who is the central point and also a good motivator is very important. In our partnership we are fortunate to have one. I hope the Training Agency will continue to support TVE for many years. Without its backing I do not think TVE will succeed. The beauty of the scheme lies in the structure of planning, executing, monitoring and evaluating and a joint effort from everyone involved. It has brought the educationalists together – between institutions, within institutions – that, in turn, will bring benefits for the pupils.

RELATIONSHIPS

Relationships with staff, non-teaching staff, pupils, parents and the community are paramount in managing an institution. I took over a staff some of whom had been in the school for more than ten years. Some of them came as probationers and stayed there. In a way it gave stability and continuity. They are good traditional teachers, caring and supportive to the pupils and to senior management. But some are set in their ways, not having any outside experience either through teaching in other schools or through in-service. It has been very difficult to move forward. In the past they were told what to do and they carried it out exceptionally well. It worked for both management and pupils. But there was no planning to meet the changes that were coming, educationally or socially. The population of the school was changing, the nature and ability range of the pupils were changing and the climate in the area was changing. Parents were more demanding – of education for their children as well as their rights.

So it was necessary to change attitudes. 'Teaching' just the subjects in the classroom was not enough. What the pupils learn, what they achieve, how they develop, had to be looked into. Were they equipped to live in a multicultural society? Have they the skills to succeed in a technological society? This had to be investigated.

In order to do this staff had to undergo training. They had to broaden their outlook, learn about the culture and tradition the pupils were bringing into school. One cannot ignore these if one wants to develop the whole pupil. Home and school have to have connecting links so that pupils do not feel isolated or find it difficult to adjust when they move from one environment to the other. To do this successfully, the curriculum and schemes of work had to be modified and developed.

We started a series of in-service courses. We consulted the staff through a questionnaire regarding what kind of courses they wanted. Two deputies, the senior teacher and myself planned the courses. We accommodated some of these within school time so that everyone benefited by the proramme. We looked at multicultural and anti-racist education, pastoral education, curriculum development, health-related issues (including information sessions on AIDS), middle management, and so on. In the last two years, on professional in-service days, we have been able to involve outside speakers and organizations. We have had sessions on education and law, stress and time management, the introduction and implementation of LMS, records of achievement and technology days. Every member of staff had a day's training with an expert on computers so that staff are not afraid to try technology. This, we hope, will encourage them to use computers in the classroom in their subject areas. We also involved members of staff from other institutions to inform us about new initiatives or any good practice in their institutions, and our members of staff have visited them. So there is lots of interaction going on that will help teachers and benefit the pupils in the long run. We evaluated the first series of courses and worked on the suggestions and criticisms that emerged.

In the beginning, the LEA's contribution to this in-service programme was minimal. They ran courses after school which some members of staff attended. Also they funded a few secondments and courses run by the DES and other organizations. Input from the Education Support Service was always available but we were reluctant to use it as its quality was not always guaranteed.

However, over the past five years, when central-government funds were made available for in-service, we have been able to have staff development tutors from Grant Related In-Service Training (GRIST). These people worked with our teachers developing new teaching techniques and material. This was most beneficial. The Local Education Authority Training Grant Scheme (LEATGS) took over from GRIST. This has given us the flexibility to use the funds and cover facilities. The staff committee responsible will now decide priorities for the development of the school and staff members. We always try to 'cascade' the information received during individual courses to the rest of the staff. Again, we try to use the funds to have a school-based course for all members of staff, sometimes including non-teaching staff and governors. We find the monies well spent. With TVE back-up funds for cover, teachers have undergone considerable training and have received more resources than ever. This has helped to develop new courses and, in many cases, change attitudes.

I was one of the fortunate ones who was selected to participate in the Local Education Authority Project (LEAP) for management training for headteachers and deputy teachers. This was a well-planned course involving videos, group work, discussion and follow-up work. We were able to criticize and evaluate the videos and the modules. The pilot videos were from suburban, all-white schools in plush, green surroundings. But we managed to change the videos and show the good work going on in inner-city multicultural schools. My school was featured in one of the modules.

One of the biggest impacts this course made on me was how I saw the school, my 'mental model', so different from how the staff saw it. The normal model is of a captain steering a ship with his or her crew (staff, pupils, parents) weathering the storm and reaching the destination. I was under the impression that everything was going well in our school and we were striving to reach the same goal. But I realized that there were some undercurrents that were diverting the course. I was glad I detected them in time and was able to avoid any serious disturbances. We started from the beginning, looking at the aims and objectives of the school, involving pupils and parents and creating the right atmosphere. By having open discussions and working in groups, we were able to work out policies for the school everyone could follow. I hope ownership of these policies will make them workable as well.

Open discussions took place with not only members of staff but also with non-teaching staff (clerical assistants, technicians and building-service supervisor). What would we do without them? Involvement of everyone – direct or indirect – is very important. The whole-school approach and an emphasis on everyone playing their role is very important.

In the second year of my headship we had industrial action by the teachers, which went on for eighteen months. I used to have regular meetings with the four union representatives. We negotiated within the guidelines. I did not want to undermine their action but made it quite clear that the safety of pupils was of utmost importance. It is so for any school, but it is more so for our type of girls living in an inner-city area. The good relationships have continued and staff have always supported the senior management, especially in times of crisis.

I prided myself on open management with consultation and involvement of staff. I did it from the very beginning but, initially, there was not a good structure and all members of staff were not ready for it. It was too soon, perhaps, for them to cope with the change and new management. The deputy heads I inherited, though supportive, were not innovative. They were happy to carry on with what they were doing. Did I not feel the same way, when the new head took over in my previous school? When I appointed my own deputies four years ago things changed. Now I feel we are all together, working for the same goal with goodwill, co-operation and support for each other wherever needed. I hope I am right this time.

One of my regrets is that, as I went up the management ladder, I started to lose contact with pupils. I had a little teaching commitment in the first years of my headship, which I have had to give up in the past two years. It was not fair on the pupils when they had to miss so many lessons because of my absence owing to attendance at various meetings. However, I cover for absent colleagues. Spending an hour without disruption in a classroom with pupils is a luxury these days.

I operate an 'open-door' policy for pupils and anyone else. Pupils are free to come to talk to me. I do not want them to be afraid of me but to respect me. They should be able to come to discuss their problems, share their concerns or happiness with me. But I make sure that they do not take advantage. Depending on what it is, I direct them through the proper channels or take action myself. I always have more patience with children than adults. I give pupils the chance to correct their mistakes and do things better, but I expect adults to be efficient and responsible. In my priority list, pupils come first. Sometimes this creates tension and misunderstanding. Of course, the pupils play one off against the other. So an effective means of communication between pupils, senior management and staff is necessary. I always try to be around the school during break times, lunchtimes and before and after school. I go round the school and look at their work and talk to pupils and staff as much as I can. Though I give freedom and flexibility to the staff to deal with certain issues, I always expect them to keep me informed so that I am aware of what is going on. As a result, most of the time the paperwork tends to be packed in the briefcase for home-work. Making pupils and staff my priority during school means paperwork and reading needs to be done at home. The working day has been getting longer and longer – an average of 12 hours per weekday, plus attendance at conferences and functions over the weekends. In the past two years paper-work has overtaken everything else. Trying to do both is not humanly possible and I have not found a solution yet.

I want the pupils to see I am an ordinary person like their parents. I talk to them about my family, my interests and hobbies and my activities during weekends or holidays. I take part in sponsored events with them, join them in community functions, visit them at home, participate in their festivals, weddings and other family events. I do my shopping in the area so that I meet them and their parents. As a result, I have very little time left for myself or my family, but isn't that true for many headteachers?

I must mention the reactions from the black community that I and many black (Asian/Afro-Caribbean) colleagues faced. In the beginning, children from our own community look at you with suspicion, judge you and assess you against white colleagues. They can be hurtful in their attitudes. But one has to prove to them that we are as good as, if not better than, our col-leagues. One has to work that extra bit harder in the beginning to establish oneself. It takes time to change the attitudes, values and, in our case, belief that white is better than black. Once you are established and have proven your worth, being black acts as a positive factor. I am very proud to be a role model for our youngsters – to tell them that they can achieve whatever they want if they really want it.

For me, parents play a very important role in the education of their children: it is a partnership between school and home. From the very beginning I made it known that parents were very welcome in school. The open-door policy existed for them as well. But parents are reluctant to come to school. Is it the school phobia many suffer as students that carries on into adult life? Asian parents have other problems as well. First, it is the tradition in Asia that education is the responsibility of the school and teachers: the parents' role is at home. Second, even if they want to come, there is in some cases the language barrier. I wanted to break this barrier. Knowing their culture, tradition and language, I was able to establish re-lationships and now they have started to visit the school.

Sometimes this positive relationship works to the opposite effect. Par-ents think because I am the headteacher I can wave a magic wand and make things happen. They want favours: allowing girls to stay at home for family reasons or taking them back to India or Pakistan on long leave. They want me to be a social worker rather than an educator.

While they want a good education for their daughters, they will not allow them to go to the library or even to their friends' houses. At home, house-work comes before homework. There are restrictions regarding field-study courses and work experience. In other words, their view of education is very narrow. I respect and sympathize with their wishes but, as a head-teacher, my first duty is to educate the girls in every way and encourage them to stand on their own feet. This is what the girls want. If the parents realize this and give their daughters enough freedom and trust, some prob-lems will be resolved.

There is a large communication gap between parents and children. It may be the language barrier, the hours the parents work, the tradition whereby children do not talk in front of adults or the influence of television and video. While parents are static (or even moving backwards, according to home-country standards), children gallop ahead. The gap is widening day by day and it is the responsibility of the schools to try to bridge this gap. As an Indian headteacher, I do it by bringing parents and children together. This is sometimes difficult and also time-consuming, but the success one has makes it all worth while: for example, a father was once persuaded to postpone his daughter's wedding until she finished her A-levels. Another time, a father was persuaded to send his daughter to the polytechnic where she wanted to go and was happy with the course, rather than to a university that was the father's choice because of its status (university is considered better than a polytechnic). I was once able to bring a husband and wife (one of my ex-pupils) together and patch up their marriage that was on the verge of break-ing up because of interference from the husband's parents. It needed pa-tience from the girl and understanding from the husband and the parents to realize that the young people had to lead their own life.

I must emphasize that what I have said is not common to all Asian parents. There are many who are supportive, who listen and co-operate. In these cases, girls are doing well both in employment and further and higher education. There are many parents who are very grateful for the help and support they have received from the school.

I am fortunate that I have good supportive parent-governors. However, party political pressures and the many conflicting demands on their time can make relationships with LEA representatives on the governing body problematic. Co-opting members from industry is an excellent idea but, for a girls school in the inner city, it is difficult to co-opt the right people. I also have great reservations regarding governors managing the school. Lack of time, knowledge and expertise may prevent them from fulfilling their re-sponsibilities. There is very little training for them and even the profession-als find it difficult to cope with all the literature that is coming out and the jargon used. So it falls to the staff and the head of the school. The delegated budget can be very effective if the governors allow the head to carry on and give real help and support and do not interfere or exercise power unduly.

PERSONAL REFLECTIONS

Despite all the hassle and pressure, I have enjoyed my headship. I must confess I enjoy the power and the status, the freedom to manage and organize, to initiate changes and develop various aspects of school life. Most of all I enjoy the contact with people – parents, members of the community, colleagues and dignitaries – and attending functions at the Council House, Chamber of Commerce and universities. Highlights include visiting St James's Palace when one of the pupils received her gold award, and attending a garden party at Buckingham Palace.

As a head, especially one of the very few Asian female heads, I have been asked to sit on various committees and address many meetings. I was a member of the Swann Committee. I have been invited by the Home Office to talk on racial harassment, by a women's unit about the role of women in high places and to talk about religious education and assemblies. I am involved in many organizations that work for better education for children from minority groups. I am one of the founder members of the Asian Teachers Association and the Black Headteachers and Deputy Headteachers National Association and have been an office bearer in both. This has given me an opportunity to meet colleagues from the black community all over the country.

I have had three opportunities to go abroad to look at the education systems in Holland, India and the USA. I was one of the delegates who attended a conference in Amsterdam on provision for migrant children. Presenters had been working on projects to develop language and vocational courses. It was interesting to see how they dealt with the education of these children. I felt that educating them as a separate group was not the answer and the British system was better. Of course, there is a difference between children of migrants in Europe and children of immigrants who have settled in the UK. There were representatives from all over Europe and some of them found it difficult to accept the idea of a headteacher from a minority group.

In 1986, with two other colleagues, I started an education exchange programme with India. We felt that our Indian youngsters had no real knowledge of their own country. So we took a group of students and teachers to India. We visited many schools and established many contacts.

We managed to travel around, not only sight seeing but also to taste the real life of India. Seeing my country through the eyes of others was a unique experience. In the past four years we have had return visits by Indian students and educationalists. I hope it will continue in the future: I am proud to be part of this project.

In 1988 I was fortunate to be selected as one of the delegates to visit Washington to look at schools in inner-city areas. The former Secretary of State, Kenneth Baker, had been impressed with these schools and what they did for youngsters from deprived backgrounds. I learnt a great deal from this visit. The schools I visited had high standards, both academic and social. There were high expectations from parents and teachers and they worked together for the benefit of the children. There was motivation and positive encouragement all the time. There was also considerable pressure on teachers and students. Examinations played a very important role and everything was geared towards them. It reminded me of the Indian education system where only academic success counted, nothing else. This was what we were afraid of, perhaps still are, with the National Curriculum. I feel there should be a balance between the two.

My priority for change has to be raising standards for all pupils, especially pupils from minority groups. To do this needs commitment, hard work and a change of attitude. Managing people who are not willing to change and who are content with doing the minimum is difficult. Being a professional, I expect professionalism from others. I expect teachers to be courteous and to keep up certain standards. It is said that senior management should encourage, praise, support and communicate with staff and boost their morale. My deputies and myself do it all the time. Don't the members of senior management need similar support? After all, they are human beings too.

A headteacher's job is more manageable if there is little or no interference from outside, and if enough time and resources are given to manage the necessary changes. It may help if someone from the office occasionally says 'well done' and encourages the head in what he or she is doing. Support from the parents and community is vital. So, too, is the opportunity for a headteacher to appoint his or her own staff! Opting out or starting a private school may be an answer to this frustration.

I was the first Asian headteacher appointed in Birmingham. My appointment attracted a great deal of publicity, coverage in newspapers and on TV and radio. There were expectations from parents, the LEA and the community. On the first day of my new term, there were four inches of snow and chaos everywhere. TV cameras were in school to televise my first day. You can imagine the butterflies in my stomach. I am glad I survived that.

In addition there were observations from politicians and LEA officers. They were proving they were equal-opportunity employers. Whichever meeting I attended, I heard a comment that they had appointed black headteachers (one at that time), a token appointment. It was their triumph. It had nothing to do with my qualifications or experience. I admit sometimes luck plays an important part: being in the right place at the right time may be true in my case. Black teachers expected special treatment from me. When they did not get what they wanted, there was much unpleasantness. It was easier to please and impress white people than the people from my community.

In the beginning, white parents looked with suspicion, and worried about their daughters eating curries, wearing sarees and speaking Hindi. Afro-Caribbean parents said they preferred white to Indian. Indians were not sure whether I would be good enough as a head. So I had to work hard – doubly hard to prove that I was a good headteacher; a good, black, headteacher; a good, black, female headteacher. I felt I was in a glass cage all the time, being watched. I felt very lonely – not one of my white colleagues because I was black, and with not many black colleagues to share my happiness or sorrow. But I did not let it deter me from fulfilling my dreams.

Twenty years ago all I wanted was to be a teacher, a successful teacher. I never dreamt I would become a headteacher, and one who made history by being the first, female, black headteacher. I am very grateful to all my colleagues, friends, parents and, most of all, pupils who helped me to fulfil my dream.

Commentary

An important factor in Rao's account is that she is an Asian woman who succeeded in becoming a headteacher. For pupils and parents from the Asian community, her appointment raised issues of confidence and highlighted potentially conflicting views between home and school. Pupils were initially suspicious, assessing her against her white colleagues. Some parents from the community looked for preferential treatment. It was, as Rao states, a hard and lonely job. But having succeeded, there are rich rewards in the successful role model she is able to provide for her pupils.

Since most of the pupils in the all-girls school are Asian, the issues of cultural differences in parents' and young people's attitudes and expectations feature prominently in Rao's discussion. Attempting to provide a good all-round education for the girls, to equip them for further or higher education or for a broad range of employment opportunities, to enable them to form satisfactory personal relationships and to take their place 'with confidence, in a rapidly changing society' must have been a daunting challenge to a new headteacher. Sensitivity and skills were needed to bridge the gap between home and the outside world and to persuade a minority of parents that education was important.

Just as important as attempts to change the attitudes of some parents were Rao's endeavours – similar to Collings' (Chapter 2) – to modify staff attitudes towards the innovations she wished to introduce. It is interesting that Rao is the only contributor who also recalls her own resistance to change and her reluctance to 'let go' when, having been acting head in a previous school, a new head was appointed. Another issue related to her previous post is the value to teachers of support from the head. This support (as Collings stresses), is vital if colleagues are to develop and to take risks and if the head is to learn to trust and delegate. An interesting issue Rao alone raises is that of different perceptions. No two individuals have the same perception of a situation. But Rao's discussion on how divergence was reduced serves to emphasize the importance, whatever the style of leadership, of having mechanisms for sharing aims and objectives.

5
Michael Evans
Trinity Church of England High School

Michael Evans qualified as a teacher from the College of St Mark and St John, Chelsea, in 1967. Thereafter, he added to his qualifications through a series of courses at Goldsmiths College, New Cross. He began his teaching career at the Coopers' Company's School, an east London grammar school, and after three years, proceeded to a large comprehensive in south-west London. In 1971 he became head of mathematics at a school in Penge in south-east London and after some years combined this with a major pastoral responsibility as senior year master in the same school. From 1978 he served as second master at a comprehensive on Epsom Downs and was appointed in 1984 to the headship of Trinity Church of England High School, Manchester, a new school that was to be established on the edge of Moss Side and Hulme and adjacent to the university and city centre.

Privilege. An enormous sense of privilege. That is the single, most compelling feeling since the day I was appointed to the headship of a new Church of England secondary school in the city of Manchester. What could be more worth while than to work in partnership with parents, governors and the wider community and to lead a team of professionals, teachers and support staff, in educating young people, in involving students themselves in that process, in raising expectations and achievement, in taking a part in the development of adolescents to the point where they are able to be autonomous and open to change in their adult lives?

This sense of privilege does not deny the frustrations of the job, its pressures, its vulnerability, its loneliness. So long as the worthiness is coupled with a long-term view and a sense of humour, a secondary head of an urban school can face with equanimity the prospect of living on the edge of a volcano. At times even that metaphor has served ill to represent the true pressures, especially within inner-city areas where the task of a head has been more like that of the Royal Engineers moving from minefield to minefield. My particular minefields have been in Manchester where I have been involved in establishing a new school and, more latterly, in consolidating its development.

THE SCHOOL

Trinity Church of England High School is a mixed comprehensive with 950 pupils on roll of ages 11–16. It is a voluntary-aided school whose trustees are the Manchester Diocesan Council for Education. Trinity was set up on the re-organization of Anglican education in Manchester and involved the closure of two smaller schools of contrasting character, each on small sites that were unable to sustain a moderate-size comprehensive.

Established at a time when Church leaders were considering the place of their schools in the maintained system, Trinity deliberately has a multi-faith and multi-denominational intake, taking pupils according to published criteria from across the city of Manchester and from elsewhere in the diocese. The school is housed in two buildings, on a single site, built in the late 1950s and in the 1960s. This accommodation was surplus to the requirements of the Roman Catholic diocese as their school rolls fell in the 1970s. The buildings were adapted and refurbished in 1984–5 to meet the needs of a new comprehensive school whose pupils would live their adult lives in the twenty-first century.

From the planning stage the opportunity was taken to include in the new school a resource base for the visually impaired. This base links with the Manchester Service for the Visually Impaired and, having begun its work in 1984 with five pupils with only moderate impairment, the base now serves thirty young people including several who use Braille, all of whom are integrated into the school's mainstream curriculum for the majority of their week.

Trinity has a genuinely comprehensive intake. It has an eclectic catchment area with no associated feeder schools but admits pupils each year from between 75 and 85 schools. A few pupils travel distances of up to twenty miles to attend the school and rather more travel the five or six miles from the suburbs in the north and south of the city. However, the great majority come from homes within a mile or two of the school and from areas of considerable material deprivation and social disadvantage.

Thirty per cent come from ethnic-minority backgrounds, over a quarter from single-parent families and about the same number receive free school meals. Nearly 30 per cent speak a language other than English at home and this represents 24 mother-tongue languages. Such a richness of variety would be difficult to match outside our larger cities.

The school was officially opened by Terry Waite in May 1986, by which time the school had established itself sufficiently well to have two applicants for every place. However, Trinity has avoided the temptation to use its over-subscription to become a quasi-grammar school and is pleased that it, in practice, recruits from across the entire social spectrum and across the complete ability range. It has admitted pupils who were unable to progress at special schools and others who have achieved the highest levels in academic attainment.

PERSONAL PHILOSOPHY OF EDUCATION

To this new school I brought a vision of education that had been developing since my apprenticeship in east London and the studies at 'Marjons' that had preceded it. A prime reason for my sense of privilege has been the opportunity to help shape a new school with my own thinking. Seminal to that thinking had been the eight years of evening courses undertaken at intervals during those twelve years when I was engaged in major curriculum and pastoral responsibilities. These courses helped me to step back and to reflect on my educational practice and the wider English school system. This combination of theory and practice equipped me with a clear view of what I wanted to establish in a school being set up in the mid-1980s. I am fortunate that these principles (my philosophy if that is not too grand a term) are best described by direct reference to what is being realized at Trinity.

I arrived in Manchester to find a whole new set of acronyms. Among these was ACS. This stood for Alternative Curriculum Strategies and seemed to be about initiatives with the older secondary pupils that were addressing the problem to do with winning back the disenchanted adolescents in the last two years of their compulsory education. It left me wanting to ask the question, 'How do we prevent losing them in the first place?' If the typical youngster is still curious and able to inquire at the end of their junior-school years, then what do we do to build on this in their early secondary years? Do we ignore the primary experience with its active learning and say, 'Sit down, shut up and listen, you are now in a proper school and engaged in proper learning'? Or do we build on that primary experience? My intention was to do the latter.

The importance of the transition at the age of 11 figures highly in my thinking. The secondary school needs to respond to the feelings of insecurity many children have during this transition. We need to organize ourselves so that pupils can develop confidence in their new setting, a confidence that will take them through the later stages of their secondary-school career. This has to be tackled in their social organization, in the physical environment and in the curriculum. Traditionally, we ask 11-year-olds to make a sudden jump to a subject-specific curriculum taught by specialists. While the examinations system at the age of 16 is mostly about discrete subjects, it does not mean that in the early secondary years, in particular, we should not be looking at the whole curriculum and be confident about approaching subjects through cross-curricular activity or through individual teachers covering several subjects. The irony is that, while we are travelling in that direction, some primary schools are moving in the opposite direction.

The significance of this transition builds on one essential tenet. It is my view that secondary education is but one phase of a life-long process of continuing education. It was not always so. When I started teaching, we thought of our courses as beginning at the age of 11. These courses were ends in themselves, with that end coming at age 15, 16 or 18. These courses did not have to concern themselves too much with what happened when the young person left school. The only exception to this would have been in relation to the small percentage of the population continuing into higher education.

There, in a nutshell, lies all that is wrong with the English system and a second principle on which I wanted to act: our over-academic curriculum. We are not prepared to value, as other systems value, the vocational alongside the academic. No single school can combat this. It is endemic in our society and our State secondary education system embraced these values in the Morant codes and regulations that followed the Education Act 1902. At that time there were examples of practice in the school system that gave esteem to the practical and even to experiential ways of learning. Those in power chose not to pursue these. Instead, it was decided – on behalf of schools – to value the theoretical and the academic. The technical and the applied was destined to have a much lower status than, for example, pure science.

A number of initiatives of the 1980s, such as the Technical and Vocational Education Initiative (TVEI), compacts and other education–industry partnerships have helped to begin to correct our value system. Broadly, these issues are to do with transition at 16-plus. To be effective in this area the school has to be open to the wider community. It has to share what it is doing. It has to be prepared to amend its practices in the light of the insights of the wider community. This is what it means to regard secondary education as but one phase of a life-long process.

It is in this context that I have a third principle as to what should govern the substance of secondary education in the compulsory school years. If we are to take a true account of what has preceded the secondary years and to develop further young people's capacity to cope with a rapidly changing technological society, then we have to adopt teaching and learning styles that are consistent with a flexible approach to learning. We have to teach young people how to learn. We have to link the curiosity and the motivation of a primary child to observe and to inquire with what we require of young adults in sixth forms, in further education, in training schemes and in employment. We have to help young people to be trainable and capable of continuing their education.

If this is to happen successfully in city schools then careful account has to be taken of factors affecting motivation – and this is my fourth principle. City youngsters are not naturally attracted by the traditional school culture. They place great store by the interest of a topic and their perception as to its relevance. They respond differently and positively if they feel valued and their self-esteem is raised. The challenge for the urban school is how to build up the atmosphere of mutual respect and common endeavour, how to develop a culture that is enlightened, caring and in which enterprise is encouraged and initiative valued. The most important place for this to happen is in the classroom, the laboratory, the studio, the gymnasium. There is no substitute for well-taught lessons and no amount of counselling or pastoral work will compensate for poor teaching. If the curriculum is right in a city school then other things will fall into place.

Central to my thinking have been the Christian notions of human worth and the inestimable value we should place on people and their God-given talents. Practices of equal opportunity and a view of education that places the learner at centre stage, seeking to develop potential in all areas of experience, flow naturally from the assertion that we are all made in the image of God. The process has less to do with what we are than what, with God's help, we might become. (The notion that we all fall short of the perfect is important on a Friday afternoon with the truculent adolescent in front of you, and equally so when things go wrong in managing the school!)

This was the philosophy of the provisional governing body of Trinity and, in many ways, it could be said that my appointment was to a philosophy, this philosophy, rather than to a school. That governing body had also determined that it would be appropriate to view the curriculum through the concept of the areas of experience HMI had been promulgating since the mid-1970s. This may seem to be a strangely relativist position for a Church school to adopt, but perhaps that says something further about the ideas behind Trinity. It was a stance I welcomed for this fitted my vision of education.

SCHOOL ORGANIZATION

Mine is not, however, a traditional view of secondary education. Schools, even new schools, have to be careful to introduce practices at a pace the community can accept. I do not believe that schools lead society. Their task is to equip young people with the capacity to change society in their adult lives. Therefore, where schools develop new practices they have to ensure that their achievements can be measured in the traditional ways. In the UK, rightly or wrongly, this means examination results and other easily collated information, such as attendance and punctuality figures or other observable features, e.g. the care of the school's environment, behaviour of pupils on buses, the amount of homework set and the appearance and general demeanour of pupils. The question for me, in 1984, was how to organize and manage the development of these principles. How was I to put these ideas into practice and prove their effectiveness by the traditional yardsticks?

I started from my classroom experience and the premise that, with very few exceptions, teachers are committed to doing a good job. They may be, as a group, cynical of new ideas but in many situations this is not unhealthy. Teachers tend not to have the same cynicism about ideas that have derived from their own work. Many of the best developments in school start from the work of teachers at the sharp end. Yet these ideas need to be given coherence and I regard it as one of the head's major roles to give a sense of direction to a school, a direction consistent with the policy laid down by the governing body.

An associated role for the head concerns staff development. This is not to be identified only with in-service training. Far more important is the system of communication, consultation and decision-making that informs and involves staff on a daily basis so that they are developing their knowledge base of what is happening in the school, their vision of education and their skills within the profession. It was these ideas that underlay the original organization of the school.

In 1984 I established a number of mega-faculties with the ambition that cross-curricular links would be more easily developed. I saw the six heads of faculty as having a crucial role as agents of change in the school and they were appointed with this in mind. These six people were to join the head and three deputies to form the school's senior management team (SMT). This would mean that every teacher would be represented in the deliberations of the SMT through their head of faculty. All that was required for this system of communication, consultation and decision-making to work was for the fortnightly meetings of the SMT to alternate with meetings of faculty teams. How my hope was dashed! Three years of the national pay dispute prevented regular meetings. The whole staff met occasionally but this required early closures of the school and therefore these meetings had to be limited in number. Furthermore, unlike the new schools of the 1960s that grew from an initial intake of pupils, we had all five year groups with us from the outset, a new first year and four inherited year groups. The early years in the school's life were, therefore, not easy and were undertaken without much consultation. I was left to address the results when I undertook restructuring in 1989.

A number of important changes had taken place in the intervening five years. The school itself was well established and had made tremendous strides. I knew, however, that further development would require a much greater direct input from colleagues and I needed to find ways of putting into practice philosophical notions to do with the enthusiasm of teachers and the ownership of ideas. Though having always attempted to avoid reference to 'my' school, it was now even more necessary for the term 'our' school to have real meaning. A number of external factors had also changed. We had a new Pay and Conditions Act with its incentive allowances. We had the Education Reform Act 1988 (ERA) and its implications, such as the National Curriculum and local management of schools (LMS) for our organization. Finally, we were about to take part in the extension of TVEI(E) and had just become one of the first Manchester schools to take part in its compact between education and industry.

The upshot was the abolition of the largest faculties in order to create smaller teams run on a traditional departmental basis. Each head of department was to be a member of the new consultative committee. They were also to be members of the school's LMS team. The new teams varied from six to eleven in number but were of a size that made formal consultation easier. Even more important they were not so large as to prevent that informal and chance consultation to take place that is so crucial to the wellbeing of a school. The obvious capacity for cross-curricular work, which was inherent in the faculty pattern, was not lost to the school for such ways of working had become part of the school's culture.

Another idea woven into the organization of the school was the link between the curriculum and its system of welfare and guidance. The original organization had included a team of year leaders who had some curriculum responsibility. The term 'year leader' had been chosen rather than head of year because I wanted to emphasize the co-ordinating and enabling role that allowed form tutors to do a better job. This is to be compared with the traditional role by which the head of year takes over the problems from form tutors as though they can be more effective with 180 than the form tutor is with their 30. That was always a doubtful proposition. In the 1989 restructuring we introduced a new tier into the system with year leaders reporting to a head of upper school and head of lower school who, in turn, reported to a deputy head (pupils). That deputy head was now to take a larger role with pupils than she had hitherto done and that in turn released me as head to develop other roles.

The school had begun with each of three deputy heads having responsibilities across the various areas of the school's life: curriculum, pastoral and administration. It was my firm belief that this was best both for job satisfaction and for career progression. I knew how important had been my own experience of having overt curriculum and pastoral posts with a smattering of administration. However, and perhaps because the new school was established without meetings, colleagues found it difficult to work out exactly who was responsible for what. In that situation, too much ended up being channelled to the head. Also we found that, although the staff development of team members featured in the job description of every postholder in the school, it had tended, in busy lives, to end up as a low priority and was simply not being tackled. In the revision, therefore, we have a deputy head (staff), who acts as a personnel manager, the deputy head (pupils) and a director of studies. These are my closest teaching colleagues, without whom I would not be able to manage the school.

The four of us form a corporate management team (CMT), which also includes four other staff with across-the-school responsibilities, these being a director of learning resources, our TVEI(E) co-ordinator and the heads of upper and lower schools. All eight of us work in close association with one another. This group meets weekly and the first item on each agenda is matters raised on behalf of other colleagues. The whole of this group is charged with the responsibility of sharing ideas with colleagues, being about the school and, above all, listening. Nothing is more important to a school staff than to see senior colleagues about the place and to know that they are being listened to. It is a sure way in which to head off problems while they are still a manageable size.

To ensure the voices of the staff are heard we now have a consultative committee that comprises the members of the CMT, all the heads of department and year leaders, holders of specific cross-curricular posts, the registrar, the senior technician and four elected representatives of other staff. This is a large group. So is our LMS team, which holds open meetings and is made up of the CMT with all the heads of department.

Local Management of Schools (LMS)

It is LMS that has led to the main changes in my role as head. Previously I emphasized the role of giving the school a sense of direction and organizing it so as to take account of staff development. Other roles included staff appointments, pupil admissions and that general task of representing the community to the school and the school in the community. As important as anything has been my role in maintaining the confidence of staff, parents and pupils in the learning environment of the school.

LMS has added to these roles. To make space I have had to delegate the school's internal day-to-day management much more effectively. In a sense that delegation is itself the management aspect of LMS, leaving decisions to be made locally, as close as possible to where they have to be implemented. The other aspect of LMS is to do with finances and resourcing. That was not new for me. Having been appointed while the architect was working on his brief, it was left for me to assume the role of project manager in a major building programme so I have always had much to do with the buildings, the furniture and equipment. Also, I have retained oversight of the allocation of capitation and other resources. LMS has meant that this responsibility has been greatly expanded with budget shares coming into school. Parts of this are being shared with teaching colleagues. But not all of the LMS role needs to be undertaken by teachers, let alone a head, and here the school has been fortunate in the quality of its support staff.

School Staff

I have no doubt that teachers are a school's single most important resource. Yet to be effective they need a professional level of support from clerical officers, technicians, caretakers, etc. The role of this group in the school's organization has, therefore, to be carefully considered. So often heads speak of 'the staff' when they in fact mean the teachers. It takes a modicum of self-discipline to refer to the teaching staff if that is what I mean so that 'the staff' is a reference to the school's whole staff, both teaching and support. It is a discipline that is well worth while. The support staff are a vital and indispensable part of the team.

The concept of teams is immensely important in the school. The conditions and service of teachers imply that all teachers, once out of their probationary period, should have responsibilities commensurate with their experience. Just as I do not run the school by myself, so no head of department should be running their department single-handedly. We have meetings of department *teams*, year *teams*, cross-curricular *teams*, corporate management *team*, always emphasizing the word 'team' with the dependency on one another this implies. A recent buzz-word has been 'collegiality'. After five years leading the school from the front I needed a vehicle for introducing the collegiality on which a healthy future for the school depends. At the time of restructuring we decided that that vehicle needed to be the school development plan.

School Development Plan

Everybody in schools is always evaluating through informal and mainly subjective ways. Here was the opportunity in the school development plan for everybody to contribute. We began with an opportunity for the whole staff to write down their aspirations for the school by completing the sentence, 'In five years time I hope Trinity will. . .'. All the responses were typed up and published. The next stage was again in a whole-staff conference when colleagues, individually or in groups, completed a SWOT analysis (writing down what they thought were the *s*uccesses, *w*eaknesses, *o*pportunities and *t*hreats facing the school). These were published and discussed by the consultative committee. Key priorities for immediate attention were identified and the rest remitted to the CMT who deliberated at a 24-hour residential conference. They returned to share with colleagues the ways in which our development plan could be effected. Through a further round of meetings we have identified four priorities from across the breadth of the school's life for the coming academic year.

In this process I have increasingly realized that heads know a great deal about a great deal but lack detailed knowledge of almost everything. They have breadth of knowledge at the expense of depth. Indeed, I find that whenever a situation leads me to take charge of the detailed execution of a task then the demands on time, energy and attention to other things prevent that task being done to my satisfaction. On the other hand, it is this breadth of knowledge that is important in giving the school its direction and that is a significant input into a school development plan.

Our four priorities are to do with pupil attitudes, staff development, records of achievement and the school's environment. The problem is that they are over and above those national initiatives about which we have no choice but to be involved. Not the least of these is the National Curriculum. But Trinity is a school in which a vast amount of curriculum development has taken place in the last six years. The school was described as a model of TVEI even before we were involved in that project. A great deal has been done in terms of teaching and learning styles, the meeting of special needs, transition from primary school and in progression from 14 to 19. How has this been organized?

ORGANIZATION OF LEARNING

True to the importance attached to the transition from primary school, we have a distinctive approach to year 7 (11-year-olds). The staffing ratio deployed for them is at least as favourable as that deployed to our year 10 (14-year-olds) and year 11 (15-year-olds). We minimize the number of teachers they meet by a single teacher covering several subjects. We base the group in one building and minimize the amount of movement required of the year group between lessons. We put 190 pupils into seven mixed-ability forms and minimize the amount of re-grouping that takes place. The purpose behind these moves has been to provide as much security as possible in an emotionally and physically demanding twelve months. However, the most significant aspect of year 7 is the style of teaching and learning, which builds on good primary practice.

A section of the week is based in our Learning Resource Base (LRB). Here the emphasis is on the development of the skills of inquiry, investigation, observation, reporting and recording. It provides a space where time can be used flexibly and topics may be cross-curricular or subject specific. The existence of the LRB has encouraged similar styles to be used elsewhere in the curriculum so that recently a visiting teacher, after touring the whole school, inquired whether anybody here taught in a traditional (presumably didactic) mode.

A visitor might expect to see active, practical and investigational styles of learning in science, technology, art, drama and physical education in any school. Trinity would be no exception except that sometimes the didactic is the best approach for a particular topic in any of those subjects. Perhaps the surprise comes when the visitor passes the religious-education groups making models, the humanities groups returning from a trail in Manchester (a wonderful resource), the music groups learning through hands-on experience of the balalaika, guitar, sitar, tabla, African drums, steel pans, etc., the English group engaged in desk-top publishing or the French group role-playing.

The fact is that the majority of teaching staff feel comfortable with a variety of styles and will use the method appropriate to the topic. I cannot emphasize enough the importance attached to having that experiential and active style as part of each teacher's armoury. The work in the LRB continues in year 8 and year 9 to encompass a rigorous approach to project-writing and the development of group decision-making and discussion skills. In year 10 and year 11 the opportunity exists for the base to be used for timetabled directed study as one of the options. Come the over-full National Curriculum, I hope it will be possible for this facility to be used for students to approach some of the attainment targets through open-learning packages.

One of the features that helped the teaching staff adopt new styles (like most teachers, we had been used to teaching behind a closed door) was our work with the visually impaired. This often required a support teacher to be in the room. It was novel to have another adult in the room. Recognizing the possibilities we began to organize our support of pupils with learning difficulties on the basis of team-teaching. Instead of withdrawing pupils, a second colleague went into the class. We began to learn much from one another and became more open to possibilities we had hitherto not considered.

Apart from our LRB and the styles of teaching, there is much on our timetable and in our school any parent would expect. As in most schools, there is tremendous pressure in year 9 (13-year-olds). Not only is the group timetabled in the LRB but also every pupil pursues a second foreign language.That is a measure of our commitment to comprehensive education. We were not prepared to reinforce the hierarchy of subjects by which the academically ablest pursue a second language while the others undertake more technology or art or whatever. This pattern has had an interesting result in that over two thirds choose to pursue a language to GCSE, a figure way in excess of other urban schools. This choice is also helped by the fact that since the school was established our year-10 (14-year-old) groups have been able to pursue up to ten subjects at examination level. It is not necessarily something we would encourage, especially given the demands of GCSE coursework. Indeed, we promote the idea of including non-examination subjects or directed study among the seven options that complement language, literature and mathematics. Yet it has provided the scope for our students to have a balanced curriculum to the age of 16. It means that we will slip quite easily into the organization required to meet the demands of the National Curriculum for that age-group.

Coincidentally, the encouragement of our academically able to include non-examination subjects in their diet has meant that these groups remain mixed ability and we therefore avoid the pitfalls and side-effects of having 'sink' groups in our upper school.

As a school we were happy to see the introduction of GCSE, even if the timing and resourcing could have been better. At a time when some schools in our local authority have pursued unit accreditation of locally devised courses, we have been content to use the GCSE system and with good effect since our results are considerably better (by a factor of 1.5) than the national averages. However, there is a gap in the provision offered by GCSE, and our participation in TVEI(E) has helped us to enhance our provision through the introduction of a Business and Technician Education Council (BTEC) course. All of these courses are complemented by what we call life skills and leisure activities.

All year groups leave with a record of achievement. We introduced 100-per-cent work experience several years ago and our involvement in the Manchester compact has helped us realize our ambition to offer mock interviews to all students at the employers' premises and to have much more face-to-face contact between students and employers in school. As more than 60 per cent of our students did, in any case, continue into sixth-form college or full-time further education, it has been difficult for many of them to see the relevance of the compact. Yet, like TVEI(E), the compact has enhanced activities that were already being pursued. They have added to the value of existing activities.

Visitors to Trinity always comment on its happy atmosphere, and our attendance figures of over 90 per cent suggest a low level of disenchantment among our students. I would want to argue that this is a direct result of our getting our curriculum right. A school will only be successful if it pays due attention to the ordinary. My experience in south-east London taught me that there is no point in pouring huge energies into a pastoral system if what is going on in the classroom in the typical working day is not of a good quality. It is in the classroom that we show, day by day, the extent to which we value our students. As noted earlier, all the counselling in the world will not overcome the effects of poor lessons. The best pastoral care is a well-taught curriculum. But not all the curriculum is planned in lesson time. In a Church school that would want to describe itself as a worshipping community it is not surprising we see our worship as complementary to the rest of our curriculum. Our worship, like our religious education, is based on a multi-faith approach though with an emphasis on Christianity. We see our worship as a celebration of all that goes on in the school, an expression of the way we value people. We endeavour, therefore, to help our students worship in ways that are relevant to them rather than imposing adult forms of liturgy upon them. Certainly we are not involved in denominational teaching or proselytizing. Rather, we aim to help young people mature in the spiritual dimension of life alongside other areas of experience.

Where teachers have worked to ensure good practice, the National Curriculum has less relevance than it might. We regard it as the *minimum entitlement* of our students. Several years on, I am able to look back on the pay dispute of 1984–7 and to recognize that while Trinity was overtly so badly affected (during an HMI inspection in February 1986 one third of our lessons needed to be cancelled) there was, behind the scenes, a great deal of effort being made by teaching colleagues to build an effective curriculum. Much depended then on the heads of faculty and course directors: it is the heads of department and, in the new structure, the three of our CMT who oversee their work and spearhead future developments. These three are our director of studies, our director of learning resources and our TVEI(E) co-ordinator. They offer a range of backgrounds and a variety of management styles. That so much has been achieved reflects well on the relationships within the school and between the school and its partners. In many ways it is good relationships that have been the key to our progress.

RELATIONSHIPS

I am not a bureaucrat. A glance in my office will show that I do not cope well with paper. Somebody kindly called it a 'working office'. My management of time is hopeless and no course on the subject has any real influence on me. I do my job by as much personal contact as possible and by building up the relationships within and about and outside the school. If I am to maintain people's confidence in the school and represent the school in the community and the community to the school – two of my most important tasks – then it is achieved through an appropriate set of relationships with parents, staff, pupils, other parts of the service, governors, churches and parishes, the wider community and business and industry. I will take each of these eight groups in turn.

Parents

Good schools have to be like good parents. They have to be both demanding and caring. Pupils spend three quarters of their waking hours at home and only a quarter at school. All parents are concerned for their children's progress but some (perhaps many) have experiences that make them find schools forbidding places. These are the reasons why schools have to seek partnership with parents and why they have to work at it tenaciously if they appear not to be succeeding. My move from urban London to its stock-broker belt broadened my experience considerably in that much of my new work was with highly articulate parents who knew exactly what they wanted from a school. Now, as head of an inner-city school, I know it is my job to encourage parents to feel a part of the school and to make their legitimate demands on us.

In 1984, I met, in turn, the parents of each of the five year groups for whom I was about to assume responsibility in the new school. The parents of the older pupils were rightly concerned that the closure of the two existing schools and the creation of the new one would disrupt their children's one examination chance. Parents in the middle of the school were concerned it would be difficult to marry the pupils from two such different school backgrounds. The parents of the youngest group knew they had applied for a school that did not yet exist and about which they had only read in a brochure. At that time it was important to meet parents, show that I had thought about the issues that would be arising and face honestly the problems I knew had no solution, while pointing out the positive aspects of the situation. Above all I intended to set the tone that schools should not act in a condescending way to parents and that schools should never adopt the stance that they are always right. I now know, with hindsight, how surprised the parents were to be taken into my confidence and how far removed from their experience was this approach.

The Trinity Association was set up in the first half-term of the school's life – such was its importance to our thinking. For two years I was its chairman but since that time all the offices have been held by parents. It is, in fact, bigger than a PTA in that all parents of existing and past pupils, staff, governors, present and past pupils and other friends of the school can regard themselves as members. It is made clear in its constitution that its primary purpose is to build up those relationships in the school that lead to a good community. It is not primarily a fund-raiser though, in the course of its functions, it may raise money. Through the association the school is open each Tuesday evening, making the school's facilities available to families and providing the chance for them to meet. By my being present, parents have a chance to mention things to me informally and without the problems of working people having to make appointments during the day. Secondary schools do not have the advantage of primary schools where so many parents meet at the gate. If we want parental involvement we have to create ways in which it can happen. The spin-off is that when problems

arise for their teenage children (as they most certainly will with adolescents) parents are able to come to the school and feel comfortable here so
that the problem can be shared between us as partners.

Now the school is established we believe this partnership commences
when small groups of parents, with their children, are shown round the
entire school prior to their making an application for a place. This is done
during the normal working day and is a task I undertake personally. Our
pupils do not bat an eyelid when we come through lessons since they are so
used to having visitors in the school. The time with prospective parents is
well spent, for they go away with a real feel for the place and with a clarity
of understanding of our vision for the school that further helps their future
involvement. Subsequently, after places have been offered, our new-intake
parents' meeting attracts a 90 per cent attendance. A typical parents' meeting during a pupil's career is attended by 70 per cent of families. The
challenge for us is how to attract the remaining 10 per cent and 30 per cent
respectively.

Meanwhile, I send school newsletters home fortnightly and encourage
parental involvement in the school's activities. A small number make an
enormous contribution of time and the majority of those with a regular
income contribute to the school's activities and extra amenities through our
charitable trust fund. Parents are always invited to come in if there is any
sort of problem. It is all time well spent. There is every indication, in this
age of marketing, that our parents do the job for us at primary-school gates.

Staff

As regards relationships with staff, I have referred above to teachers being
the school's single most important resource and the need for them to
receive a professional level of service from support staff. I have met governors who have commented that the most important role they have is to
appoint a head when a vacancy occurs. Similarly, I regard my part in the
appointment of colleagues as crucial to the school's well-being. Once
people are in post, it is my intention that I should not be a remote figure. I
attend our morning briefings and try to be available to colleagues, given
that the day-to-day running of the school is largely delegated. As with
parents, it is most important that staff should feel they can see the head if
that is what they most want. I know we are not a small school but we have
attempted to cultivate a climate where information is exchanged, in a
small-school way, person to person, informally, on corridors in passing if
necessary. Even so, I am accused of destroying a small forest with the

amount of paper that passes around. Being about the school is important. You see at first hand what is happening even if the view is like that of the police patrol car on the motorway. If something is not quite right it is very often enough for it to be known that you, as head, know. Some people refer to this as management by walkabout. Where situations cause concern and a colleague needs challenging, then this is best done directly and without 'beating about the bush'. However, such discussions can be fraught and heads can never be sure that what will be recounted in the staff-room bears much relationship to what has been said.

In six years I have been surprised at how much suspicion, verging on hostility, there is among teachers in the system as a whole concerning head-teachers. It was not something I had met to any great extent in my previous local authorities. I knew that almost all teachers enjoy their moan, and what better target than the head? As a classteacher, I had been as loud as anyone. Perhaps it was the decade, but it took five of my six years in post to reach the point where almost all staff trust my motives and my leadership. I have never attempted to work charismatically, but neither have I had to make redress to my status and position for the authority that the school's articles of government give me. Rather, I have based authority on the knowledge and understanding I have gained from my experience. Similarly, one of my tasks is to ensure for my colleagues that *their* skills are developed, *their* careers enhanced and that job satisfaction is found by them.

If this is to happen they need to be valued and treated as individuals. It is noticeable in Trinity that the 50 per cent of our students who bring some sort of social or emotional hurt with them to school are mirrored by those staff whose life experience has included some sort of domestic, social or emotional problem. I am privileged to know a little of everybody's background and the problems they have encountered in life. I hope I take account of people's individuality when I am observing and informally assessing their contribution. There will always be some in schools for whom the task is a way of life, while others have a clear demarcation with full lives out of school and many interests. Both types are needed in a school. It was never valuable for a teacher to look over his or her shoulder and think how little that other person does compared with them. When that starts happening it is time to get out of teaching. It is not a job people undertake primarily for its financial rewards. Almost any job would have to be easier for the income involved. The commitment and dedication so many teachers and support staff give a school is humbling in itself and is a good starting-point for the relationship between a head and the other staff of a school.

Work with young people needs to be creative. Heads have therefore to afford every opportunity for teachers to be creative, to think up their own ideas and to be encouraged to develop them. Creative people in any field can be difficult to manage. One seems to be the price of the other. Similarly, in urban areas schools attract young committed teachers. Almost by definition those teachers will be politically (small 'p') aware and active. Again, they can be difficult to manage. I can only say, as I have had cause on occasions to say to our governors, give me the committed, creative teacher any day and I will cope with the management problems.

My style of management has been to encourage flexibility, divergent thinking and the lateral approach that today's schools need if our pupils are, in turn, to be prepared to cope with change. Schools, their organization and their curriculums, are highly complex. The DES is finding this in its efforts to fit the whole of the National Curriculum into the school pattern. At the school level that curriculum is but one of several time-consuming initiatives. Treating people as cogs in machines will not see these activities developed. There is far too much scope for sabotage in the classroom. Progress depends on the professionalism of teachers, their goodwill and an attitude that provides scope for them to develop themselves and their enthusiasms. Therefore, I do not seek to run a tight ship but rely heavily on that professionalism and on my good working relationships with colleagues.

Pupils

Many of the starting-points for those good relationships with staff are replicated in a head's style with pupils. The friendly 'hello', the eye contact, the smile, all set the tenor for what needs to be mutual respect. Pupils need to know they matter and that people should be valued for who they are rather than what they are. I find it important to talk to pupils around the school, to see them and be seen by them in corridors, dining halls, recreational areas and lessons. It is important to support their sport, music, drama and other extra-curricular activity and to be aware of the lives they lead outside school. It is useful in a city with two soccer teams to share the rivalry and the ribaldry this creates. It helps that I know so many of their parents. It helps that I live in the city and am seen by pupils shopping. It helps that my own children are in the school and that their friends are friends of our family.

This means that pupils feel they can come directly to my office with a problem, and some do. It also means that on those rare occasions when I raise my voice they know I mean business. It means that on those even rarer occasions when a pupil is excluded that it is not the result of personal vendetta but something genuinely deserved. They will also know that even when this extreme is reached we still care for them as individuals. And that is a most important example to set, a most important tenor to establish in a Church school in an inner-city environment. Some young people need much understanding and unless someone is prepared to put in the time on them their energies will become destructive rather than constructive. Heads need to be numbered among the great many staff who give freely of their time in this way.

Other Parts of the Service

Relationships with groups outside the school can also play a vital part in its well-being. There are the other local schools, which regard us as rivals. It has been crucial that we be seen to play a full part in the system, sharing in solutions to its problems. At a personal level, the contact with other heads is a great source of mutual support. Also, the officers and members of the local authority and diocese, members of the local inspectorate or HMI, professional colleagues in the other caring sectors all have a part to play. My experience tells me that the more you recognize and value their contribution, the more they will help a school. I have never felt threatened by people in the service but outside of schools. It is helpful to know that we have distinctive jobs but are all working to the same end, the best education for children. We will sometimes disagree as to the means to that end but it is wise to remember that it is only disagreement on means and not ends.

Certainly, Trinity could not have been established in the way it was without a huge input from the specialist skills of officers in the authority. We sometimes refer to our senior secondary inspector as having been the school's midwife. All other inspectors showed a great enthusiasm for the school and a willingness to help its establishment in whatever way was possible. Our local HMI made contact during my early days in the post and headed up a week's inspection of the school just a few weeks after our practical provision was completed and before we were officially opened. Their comments were constructive and helpful and I believe it is valuable for a school to receive an outsider's view of the school from fellow professionals with the experience and expertise of HMI.

Governors, Church and Parish

The position of governors in an aided school has always made them inclined to be involved. They have always been the employer, they manage the building and they have always been responsible for the curriculum. Having been appointed as a head who shared their vision, I know they have wanted to leave the management of its implementation to me. The converse is that I know their mind and would only promulgate a course of action that might cause disagreement after long and careful thought. In six years that has not happened. I feel the school receives great support from its governors. Certainly they give up a considerable amount of time on school work related to admissions, appeals, buildings, staff appointments, curriculum issues and other general and financial matters.

All of our governors form links with the community. Our foundation governors, in particular, form links with individual parishes, deaneries and other parts of the diocesan organization. It was important on our establishment that the 87 potential parishes we serve should feel that in some sense or other we are 'their' school. I, therefore, write an occasional newsletter to the parishes, preach from time to time in local churches and this contact is supported by the musical groups from the school who perform at regular intervals in parishes across the archdeaconry. The Diocesan Synod meets in school. All of this contact is important. We are not what the typical person in the pew expects a Church school to be. There is much about our admissions agreement and our educational practices that could cause controversy, and it is better that we make the moves towards the parishes.

Community, Business and Industry

Our links with the wider community are more of a problem. What does community mean when students come from the length and breadth of a city the size of Manchester and others come from beyond its boundaries? Yet we are in a unique position for we are in a city with its own north–south divide, and many of our families do not really know that part of the city from which they do not come. We have no clear strategy at the minute other than to share whatever we can of the city's life and to be involved even-handedly in north, centre and south. We are located in the centre and we regard our local neighbourhood as Hulme, Moss Side, the university and the city centre itself. This local neighbourhood is rich in resources and from that point of view the school is ideally located. Our links tend, therefore, to be with people who can help us with resources or to whom we can be a resource. Industry and commerce are a very special category within this group.

Three years into the life of the school we were sufficiently well established for me to begin making those contacts that are so vital to a secondary school whose pupils will eventually be seeking employment. I found employers were pleased to be invited in. In many ways, their knowledge of education had stopped with their own schooldays and they were not only surprised by what they saw but, having heard so many negative things about education in the media, were also delighted at the opportunities the school was offering. I recall one explaining that he had not been sure what to expect but thought it likely it could be 'organized mayhem'. He was kind enough to observe that it was far from being like that. Another reckoned that managers could learn a great deal from the relationships he had seen in lessons. This particular chief executive thought that most industrial relations in the UK were largely based on a master/pupil model of a bygone age and schools had changed, leaving industry behind.

Each contact has been able and keen to introduce me to their associates. Thereby the school's business network has expanded rapidly and, with it, the number of employers who were prepared to help the school in some way or other. The Manchester compact has furthered this work and provided fresh links. Meanwhile, several of the original group have been co-opted to our governing body and they add a fresh dimension to its proceedings. These particular people are closely involved in the regeneration of Manchester. One of the recurring themes in our school has to do with Manchester's growth, decay and subsequent regeneration. It has been fortuitous that there has been a growing optimism in our city since the mid-1980s, an optimism of which we feel a part.

PERSONAL REFLECTIONS

Trinity was fortunate in being established at the time it was. Timing has been important in the achievements we have accomplished. There is a feeling of satisfaction in setting up a truly comprehensive school. Moreover, we have maintained a comprehensive character and avoided the potential abuse of over-subscription to become a 'middle-class bolt-hole'. We remain a hard middle-class choice because of our geographical location. We are not a soft option and that is our strength. Some parents have to overcome many prejudices before sending their children to us, and there is a sense in which we are flying a flag for the maintained sector against the independent sector of education. There is equal satisfaction in our being recognized as a beacon of good practice in urban education and the fact that we showed 'faith in the city'. We have been an open school and have been pleased that people have been sufficiently interested to visit us.

I know that headship has used all the variety of my past experience and now, six years on, I take great satisfaction in seeing colleagues develop their experience and in knowing how the contrasting backgrounds of the two previous schools have been fused into a new setting and philosophy, the staff blending together and working as a team.

So much for the aspects that are satisfying. The part of the job I least enjoy is paper, that is, other people's paper! The telephone is another weapon of those who would destroy a plan for the day. It takes an iron will to prevent life becoming like the 'in-tray exercises' beloved of management courses. On the wider front there is also a continuing degree of economic uncertainty for the service in a high-spending local authority. Indeed, there is a general frustration in sitting between national and local governments of different political hues. The job has enough pressures and complexities without that particular one. There is always the personal tension to do with the use of time and the extent to which I step back, distance myself and have the possibility to evaluate and reflect. This conflicts greatly with the need I feel to keep myself involved and thereby keep the role of maintaining the confidence of staff, parents and others in the school. This is the tension that exists for many heads. Are you the school administrator or are you the leading professional? I hope the description of my task at Trinity makes my answer to that abundantly clear. It is this passion for education and respect for its professionals that helps me recognize our shortcomings.

The most important changes that would make the job easier relate to the morale of teaching staff and the level of stress they exhibit. It seems to me that morale can be talked up or talked down. This can happen both inside and outside of schools. It would do much for every school if the government were consistent in its recognition of the value of teachers. No clearer signal could be given than for ministers themselves to use the maintained system. Apart from that move there needs to be a much greater recognition by central government of the overload of the system and the stress this is creating among teachers. One could be forgiven for thinking that the pace of change has been deliberately set to create maximum damage to the maintained system of education that, in some people's eyes, was being far too successful in raising the expectations of young people.

Some teacher stress could be lowered by an increase in the number of support staff so as to conserve more teacher energies for actually teaching. Another way forward is the school development plan, which is a significant way in which priorities can be ordered. School staffs do not find it easy to distinguish between the vital and the highly desirable, but only if we do so can we make manageable the pace of change. Other stresses come from physical surroundings. The physical environment of a school is important and the wrong environment creates unnecessary stresses.

Any help with improving the status and morale of teachers has to be useful for those of us who are addressing issues of management in schools. If we are ever to have an effective education service, we need well-motivated teachers with high expectations. And it is from among the ranks of those teachers with successful and varied classroom teaching experience that I hope heads will continue to be appointed. The headship of a school is not predominantly an administrative function. Of the roles of headship, many are to do with working at the boundaries of the school. Yet not everything is peripheral and, of these, nothing could be more crucial than the head's role in motivating and leading a professional team.

Heads are not so different from the team of classteachers they lead: the constant exposure to the demands of others can be hard work; the hours are long, but still there is not the time to do all that one would wish; one can be wrestling with less than adequate resources; or perhaps trying to marry irreconcilable tensions and differences. One is involved in structuring the work of, and the motivation of, others, and the results depend on the maintenance of high expectations. Much is similar. Only the scale is different. And that includes the stresses, the vulnerability and the loneliness.

As teachers progress in the profession, their sphere of influence increases. The size of the canvas on which they are operating increases in proportion to responsibility. It might be thought that this is to do with power but that is not the case. I had more immediate power when I was head of mathematics and senior year master than I have experienced since. Good middle managers in schools, with their close contact with staff and pupils, are able to implement ideas very quickly if they have the will so to do. Heads of large schools cannot do this to any significant degree. Heads can only achieve what they lead others in achieving.

Rather than power, the role of the head has to do with influence. So I return to the notion of privilege. For it is a privilege to be able to influence a school and its community, to have a vision of education and the possibility of realizing it. To be successful, heads have to take a long-term view. They have to be able to ride out short-term and local difficulties. They have to recognize what the situation is and what it might become. If visions are ever to become realities then they have to value the ordinary. Above all else, they have to value all those people who are partners in the process of education. They have to be able to operate with them in teams, leading from different positions according to the situation. Whatever the particular style, heads remain the school's leading professional. Herein lies the privilege that is headship.

Commentary

Evans is concerned about the transition from primary to secondary school
– an issue he addresses in terms of social organization, physical environment and curriculum. For Evans, this transition is a key factor in his view of
education as a flexible system of life-long learning.

Christian belief is also important for Evans, leading, as he does, a
diocesan-wide, multi-faith and multi-denominational school. Most contributors' concerns are to promote equality of opportunity, albeit for a
variety of reasons. Evans is keen to do so because of his belief that 'we are
all made in the image of God'.

Like Flecknoe (Chapter 3), Evans considers the staff to be a school's
single most important resource. Developing their skills and enhancing their
careers, he believes, is an important task of headship. He does, however,
raise the sensitive issue of how best to manage teachers who are young,
committed, creative and politically aware and active.

The issue of teacher morale, raised already by Flecknoe and Collings
(Chapter 2), is commented on by Evans, who calls for the government to
recognize the value of teachers and to show more support for the maintained system. While acknowledging the privilege of headship, Evans does
not deny its difficulties. He comments on 'the pressures, the vulnerability
and the loneliness' of the job.

6
Bryce Leggatt
White Oaks Secondary School

Bryce Leggatt obtained a BA degree at McMaster's University, in Ontario, in 1964 and qualified as a teacher a year later at the University of Toronto. He has held posts in several schools in the Halton Board of Education, Ontario. From being head of physical education he went on to become a vice-principal and, in 1981, principal of a high school. Since 1985 he has been principal of White Oaks Secondary School. As an educational leader, Leggatt has been instrumental in introducing social workers and guidance counsellors into schools and in designing an authority-wide policy on race and ethno-cultural equity. Bryce Leggatt is married with two children.

THE SCHOOL

Recently, White Oaks Secondary School celebrated its twenty-fifth anniversary. This occasion provided a welcome opportunity to reflect on the development of our school. We are proud not only of the rich tradition that has emerged over this first quarter of a century of our existence but also of the school itself.

White Oaks is one of six high schools in Oakville, a suburb of Toronto with a current population of approximately 100,000. The town is growing rapidly and is projected to double in size in the next twenty years. It is one of a number of communities in the region of Halton. Approximately 30 kilometres west of Toronto, the region not only serves as a dormitory community to Toronto but also has its own base of light manufacturing industry. With the influx of people, especially to Oakville, there has been a

107

rapid growth in population and a significant increase in its diversity: the racial and ethno-cultural composition of Halton is changing dramatically, and this change is one of the principal features our school has had to contend with in recent years.

When it opened in 1965, White Oaks served a mostly rural population and, of the 700 students who entered that year, over two thirds were transported by school bus. Since then, the school population has grown steadily, particularly as urban growth spread west from Toronto. More and more of the area around the school was developed so that, by the early 1970s, two thirds of the students were walking to school while only one third continued to be bused.

White Oaks, with over 1,700 students, is the largest secondary school in the Halton Board of Education, a jurisdiction (LEA) that comprises Oakville, the city of Burlington and the towns of Georgetown, Milton and Halton Hills. Halton Board serves 43,000 students in its 66 elementary schools and 17 high schools (secondary schools in Ontario serve students primarily between the ages of 14 and 19).

When I arrived at White Oaks in 1985 I inherited a school with 1,300 students and a reputation for being academic. The surrounding community could now be described, in economic terms, as a middle-class community. Oakville, on the whole, is recognized as one of the wealthier communities in Canada, although that does not reflect the basic make-up of the area around White Oaks.

In the years I have been at the school there have been many changes. Some of these were organizational or structural, and some have emerged from our efforts to be a more effective school. I will first describe briefly the organizational changes, for they precipitated some of our measures to improve the quality of our educational effort. The initial changes made in the school during my tenure were to do with the organization of the school. They were undertaken primarily because there was a clear indication from staff, students and the community that changes were not only needed but were also likely to be readily accepted and welcomed. By undertaking these changes I would meet expectations and, at the same time, enhance the opportunity to build trust between the staff and myself. Clearly, if trust is to emerge one has to prove oneself trustworthy. By focusing on what to me were fairly straightforward issues expressed by the various parties, I was able to forge quickly a good relationship with the staff.

STRUCTURAL AND ORGANIZATIONAL CHANGES

The first change of any magnitude was the implementation of semestering. Semestering is a system whereby students enrol for a concentrated programme of only four or five subjects for one half of the year. They complete those courses within the half year and then begin a second programme of four or five courses, in the second half of the year. Noticeable features of semestering are that the length of periods in the school day are longer (in our case, 79 minutes); students study only four or five courses at a time; staff are responsible for the preparation and marking of only three courses at a time; and the school year, in effect, begins and ends twice between September and June. Previously the school had been organized on a two-day cycle. This meant that at any given time the students were responsible for all eight or ten of their courses and the staff were required to prepare for six classes within each two-day period across the school year.

The implications of semestering as opposed to those of a yearly operation have been debated endlessly in Ontario. It is worth noting, however, that over 80 per cent of the secondary schools in the Province of Ontario are now semestered, in spite of the fact that the system was only introduced in 1970. The longer periods provide students with the opportunity for more in-depth study of their courses – particularly advantageous to programmes that are practical or have a hands-on aspect to them. The other advantage, as we see it, is the realization for young people that there is an end in sight. Consequently we can talk in terms of short-term goals and we can help them to see their way through a course to the end of the semester. This is not to suggest that there are no advantages in a year-long operation – there are, but all in all we were ready to proceed with a semestered pattern.

We went through a process of providing information for students, staff and parents and of soliciting feedback as we proceeded to study the prospect of semestering. In the course of four months we received overwhelming support from all three groups and were encouraged to go forward with it. Alongside semestering came concomitant changes in many of our policies, practices and procedures: for example, attendance and lateness-reporting procedures had to be altered; field-trip practices were changed; and reporting to parents was radically revised. Staff committees took major responsibility for the design and implementation of semestering and for the resulting alterations in our practices. This process set the tone for what was to come. At this point the message was clear that I was prepared to share, not only with the leaders in our school (our heads of departments), but also with the teaching staff, the authority for making changes in our school and for designing a school we thought best served the White Oaks community.

We evaluated the students' response to semestering at the end of the first year. Results were interesting for two reasons. First, the majority of students, particularly students in grades 9 to 12, liked the system, preferring it to the previous one. Second, our senior students (called grade-13 students at the time; there are now no grade-13 students in Ontario) were troubled by semestering for one oft-repeated reason: they claimed that they had to 'work too hard'. Under the previous system, where classes occurred every other day across the year, they found they could procrastinate – putting off homework and assignments and even avoiding them completely (particularly when holidays or long weekends interfered with the two-day. cycle). Semestering allowed no opportunity to 'get around' the daily requirement of homework and study.

CURRICULUM

At the same time as the changes mentioned above, we began to address the curriculum. Previously, curriculum choices for students, particularly senior students, were narrow, even though Ontario secondary schools have the authority to offer a wide and diverse range of courses at senior level. There are some core requirements, but there is also the opportunity to provide students with a variety of options to enhance their programmes of study and to focus them towards specialization as they consider graduation, work or higher education. Consequently, White Oaks was losing a number of students each year to other secondary schools in our region. Hence we began to broaden curriculum choices and to look at other ways of packaging and presenting our offerings.

Initially, modular courses in social science were introduced; improved field-trip opportunities were developed; and twinning with schools in other countries, such as Japan and the USA, was extended. The Japanese scheme was a particularly rewarding accomplishment, which took over two years to achieve. White Oaks is now twinned with Neyagawa Furitsu High School in Neyagawa, a suburb of Osaka. Recently we completed all the necessary arrangements for exchange, enabling ten of our students to travel to Japan to the school for a period of two weeks. The Japanese students are scheduled to return to stay with us, sharing in our high-school experience and seeing the sights and special features of southern Ontario.

At present, schools in Ontario are organized on a system of levels. There are, essentially, three levels: basic, general and advanced. Schools can also provide an enriched programme and, although such programmes are not identified as a level according to the Ministry of Education for Ontario, many high schools in the province choose to do so. Basic-level programmes are those designed for students who are focusing on vocational education and who, upon graduation, will be entering work. General-level courses are designed for the majority of students in our high schools who, after graduation expect to proceed to community colleges or into employment. The advanced-level programmes are designed to prepare students for university, although some graduates from these programmes do proceed to community college and/or employment.

At White Oaks we have enhanced and diversified our enrichment programmes to meet the needs of our gifted and talented students. We made initial links with the vocational school across the street from us so that we might serve our students and theirs more effectively. A cross-registration process was put into place so that our students, who were interested in and suitable for programmes at the vocational school, could take these courses while maintaining their registration at White Oaks. At the same time, students in the vocational school could take advantage of this procedure. For many students, particularly those at White Oaks, it made entry to the vocational setting more acceptable. At present we have almost 150 students in the two schools who are taking advantage of this process.

SHARED DECISION-MAKING

You will have noticed that, in the course of this description, I have referred frequently to 'we'. All that is described above and all that follows is the result of a collective effort by the school administrators (principal, vice-principal and heads of departments) as well as the teaching staff, support staff and others. The use of appropriate language is, I think, important. Staff, students and the community need to understand that this is not 'my' school but 'our' school. In my view the language of change is an important element in conveying to all one's intent and commitment to a collaborative process. In the five and a half years I have been principal of White Oaks I have made only one arbitrary decision, and that was to ensure that our reporting process to parents would include three full reports each semester. The irony is that, among the hundreds of decisions that have been made at White Oaks in my tenure, this remains one of the most disliked by the teaching staff. None the less, it has improved our communication with parents and students and has gone a long way towards eliminating criticism of the lack of information about students' evaluation.

The present-day principal faces many diverse expectations, and the demands of the role are increasingly complex. None of us has all the

answers, nor should we be expected to solve problems without considerable help. Further, research clearly suggests that the more leadership is
shared with a responsible group, the more effective, more acceptable even,
can be the decision-making and the problem-solving.

We have taken a number of steps at White Oaks to involve staff. From
the beginning of my tenure we began an intensive training programme for
heads of our departments. Our heads of department team (or cabinet)
comprises the staff member in charge of each organizational unit in our
school, such as mathematics, English, social sciences – thirteen in all. In
addition, two vice-principals and myself are members of the cabinet. We
make up the group that takes all decisions with respect to school policy and
procedures. There are three exceptions to this practice, as follows:

1. The day-to-day decisions made by school administrators (principal and
   vice-principals) concerning the daily operation of the school, student
   discipline and the supervision/evaluation of the teaching and support
   staff.
2. Cross-school curricular issues that are addressed by a team of teachers
   called the programme planning team.
3. School goals and our school plan, which are designed and directed by
   our goals committee.

The heads of departments and administrators have worked hard at understanding the expectations relating to group decision-making and in applying them to each situation in the school. We have created a handbook of
procedures for the operation of meetings, and all decisions that have been
enacted during my time at the school have been made through consensus: I
cannot remember a vote ever having been taken. Major decisions in the
school, such as budget and the allocation of time in the planning process for
the coming year, are collaborative decisions made by the cabinet. Give and
take continues to astound me, and the willingness of all to seek the best
possible decision is an aspect of this school I will never forget.

Of course, one of the features of this method of leadership is that things
do not always 'go your own way'. This approach requires trust and respect.
As a school administrator I have to be willing to give credibility to any
suggestion, idea or approach. This is not to say it will be accepted (given
the process described above), but it will be heard and there will be a
response. The integrity of ideas, points of view and the individual is, then,
respected and, in turn, a mutual respect between the leadership of the
school and the staff emerges.

After the first year and a half of the implementation of semestering, we
began to plan for the future. The wealth of information and research in the

field of school planning offered a limitless number of approaches and alternatives. Our school system was only at the early stages of its work in this area, and we felt some urgency to proceed, so we began to work towards the design of the White Oaks school plan or, as it is now known, the White Oaks School growth plan.

SCHOOL PHILOSOPHY

It soon became clear to us that it was important we should determine what White Oaks was all about. What does the school stand for as a large composite school serving north Oakville? What does its staff value and, for that matter, what do the students value? What are the expectations of this community for its children, and can the school deliver them? These questions (and many more) had to be addressed. It became apparent that a school plan should emerge not only from a statement of school philosophy specific to the particular school but also from an in-house design that reflected the quality and characteristics of the school and its community, as well as the teaching staff and its students. This does not mean we could ignore the research or the other supports available, but it does touch on what we believe are the most critical functions of any school growth plan.

First and foremost, I believe, an effective school should be able to identify what it believes in and what it values. Accordingly we organized a committee of four that included one of the vice-principals, a parent, a head of a department and a teacher, to draw up a statement of school philosophy. This committee worked for seven months on the design and draft of this statement. They received numerous submissions and ideas from interested staff, parents and members of the community. I made a submission that was considered equally with all the others. In May 1987 the statement of philosophy was presented to the staff in draft form. A number of suggestions for modification and change were made but it was clear that, even with this initial presentation to the 77 teachers on the staff at the time, the statement had found some common ground. After re-working it once again it was presented to the staff in June 1987, whereupon it was unanimously approved by all teachers and administrators in the school:

THE PHILOSOPHY OF WHITE OAKS SECONDARY SCHOOL

White Oaks Secondary School recognizes that students are the basis of its existence. We believe formal education has a significant impact on the development of the individual. We seek to develop in our students self-esteem and heightened self-awareness through success-oriented learning and co-curricular activities within a school environment which fosters mutual respect and tolerance, which values individual differences, and which is free of fear, coercion, harassment, and prejudice. We are committed to providing equal opportunity for all students.

Students are encouraged to pursue excellence by setting and achieving challenging goals commensurate with their abilities. Instruction, then, focuses on the development of skills, abilities, knowledge and attitudes which will allow students to fill adult roles successfully in a rapidly changing world, and to benefit from further training and education after they leave White Oaks.

We view discipline as an essential component of an effective school. It will be maintained according to a code which outlines clear expectations of student behaviour and logical, fair consequences of inappropriate behaviour. This code is developed by representatives of the entire school community. Its goals are the development of self-discipline and the protection of individuals from physical or psychological harm. We recognize that some trial and error accompanies maturation: therefore, disciplinary measures involve the student in problem-solving for behaviour correction.

All students will have opportunities to develop a feeling of ownership in the school through participation in decisions which affect them and through sharing in the responsibility for creating and maintaining positive school climate.

The relationship between White Oaks and our local community will be a close and mutually beneficial one with a sharing of facilities, programs, and resources. Students are encouraged to make a commitment to societal participation through an emphasis on involvement and citizenship within both the school and the community. White Oaks recognizes its responsibility to the larger society of which it is a part to aid in transmitting our Canadian heritage and fostering global awareness.

White Oaks Secondary School views its role in the educative process as an honour and pledges the commitment of all its staff to providing a caring, supportive, high quality learning environment for the students whom it services.

This statement is not uniquely thought-provoking. What is different and special, though, is the realization that all staff endorsed the document. Consequently it has become an important tool in the process of developing a school plan and other activities in which we engage during the course of the school year (for example, when we hire and promote staff). In other words, it really has become the organizing policy for our school plan.

THE SCHOOL PLAN

Since the two vice-principals and myself were breaking new ground, at least for us, we felt it necessary to design a model and work from that model towards the plan. Some of the key concepts we wanted to include in it were the cornerstones upon which we intended to build. In our case it became evident that the cornerstones should be the values we identified in our statement of school philosophy. On reading the statement you will have noticed that each paragraph refers to the four major building-blocks of the plan. They are

- instruction
- curriculum
- climate
- community.

We hope there is a consistency between the major features of our plan and those features stressed in the research into effective schools. However, it was important to us to realize that we had come to the identification of these qualities through an internal process that was unique to our school and our sphere of control.

Another important feature of our model is its simplicity. It has to be a communication tool as well as serving an organizational function. We wanted to ensure that, through the publication and presentation of this model, we could make it clear to staff, students and the community what our school plan was all about. It should be evident that we were focusing on four key areas and that the model would centre on two key concepts: 'learning and achievement for all' and 'a challenging and supportive environment'.

A third aim in building the school plan or, more specifically, the model, was to create some sense of motion, of activity. To this end we settled on a circular design that not only created this sense of movement but also more closely tied the interdependent parts together. It was also easy to attach specific dates or a schedule of dates to it. These time frames became the intervals we used on an annual basis for the planning, preparation, publication, review and evaluation of our accomplishments.

We decided our plan should follow a one-year cycle and the circular format created that notion more readily. The one-year format also forced us to report regularly to all concerned about success or failure in achieving our goals. In addition, as we evaluated and reported to the staff and the community at the end of the school year, we could decide to continue with a particular goal or move on to some other. This re-focusing might emerge as a result of the evaluation that had just taken place and the various pressures or initiatives that had emerged from our board office or other sources.

The planning model is outlined in Figure 6.1. The whole exercise is administered and organized by a goals committee consisting of the principal, a vice-principal, a parent, student representatives from key student organizations in the school and staff representatives from important staff organizations and other departments in the school. As principal, I have no more influence on this committee nor its deliberations than any other member.

The most important decision the goals committee makes is determining the goals for the coming school year. With information in hand from the evaluation of the previous year (concluded in June) and input from a variety of different sources in the school (for example, programme planning team, student council, principal), the goals committee describes a goal for each of our four areas of focus. This process takes place in late August and early September so that, by our first staff meeting at the beginning of the school year, our school goals are clearly stated and each group and interested party in the school can begin to set out plans of action to fulfil them.

In the year of writing, for example, we had over thirty activities aimed at the realization of these goals. Activities are submitted to the goals committee in September and at our staff meeting on the first Monday in October a finished plan is presented to the staff. At the same time it is made available to parents, students and the community at large. There is clear evidence that school goals and activities have a better chance of success when they are clearly articulated and regularly referred to by the school. I use parents' evenings and other opportunities to refer to our plans and activities so that the community is constantly reminded about what we are setting out to achieve through the year.

Figure 6.1   White Oaks Secondary School planning model

An interim review is conducted in January and, at the end of our first semester in late January, a report is made to the staff updating our progress. Finally, in May, all the necessary information and background support is gathered to complete a final report that is compiled and submitted to the staff in late June. During each of the last few years we have gone through an independent exercise designed to evaluate the effectiveness of our plan, particularly to evaluate such higher-order qualities as collaborative decision-making, collaborative planning and instruction and climate.

An effective evaluation of a school growth plan is vital. We wanted to know what the parents, students and staff thought of our school and our efforts, as articulated in the plan. We also wanted to know if the plan was making any real difference. For the parents we used a printed report card. This was sent home at the end of the school year with their son's or daughter's report. The format was simple, requiring only a tick on a check-off list, although there was space for comments. I devised an incentive for parents to return this by offering a free dinner for two at a local restaurant. However, the response was disappointing: just over fifty reports were returned. In one family both the husband and wife responded, fairly I thought, but possibly with the hope that they might improve their chances of winning the dinner. Unfortunately their name was not drawn! The feedback we did receive was very helpful and one of the major issues it raised was communication. Most of us in education have heard this phrase before. None the less, we set about in our subsequent school plan to improve on this area.

In order to obtain feedback from the students we repeated a survey developed by a university academic, which I had carried out when I first entered White Oaks. Thus we had some baseline information against which to assess responses.

The initial evaluation method to be conducted among the staff had to consider a number of factors, not least of which was ease of completion and acceptance. One had to bear in mind that surveys and questionnaires completed at the end of a lengthy school year are not always welcome. As a result, we decided to use interviews. I obtained the help of the co-ordinator of research on our school board and hired an independent interviewer to work with her. The research co-ordinator has a wealth of information and a broad background not only from our board but from further afield. The other interviewer was a retired secondary-school teacher from the Halton region. He had little (if any) prior knowledge of our plan and was not at all familiar with White Oaks Secondary School. The questions they devised and the responses they elicited effectively measured our success, as perceived by the staff, and provided me with honest and clear information. The following are some of the comments we received in answer to the final question, 'Will White Oaks' plan make it a more effective school?':

- 'There's a lot of it going on . . . it will involve everybody with the task'.
- '. . . because of the involvement of teachers'.
- 'It gives people direction'.

PROGRAMME PLANNING TEAM

At the outset of this chapter I referred to three groups in the school who have had a major responsibility for the school's direction. I have already described the role of the heads–administrators as well as that of the goals committee: the third group is the programme planning team. This is a group of interested staff, one per department as a minimum, who have assumed responsibility for cross-school programmes. This team was created for a number of reasons. First, it is apparent to me that a large school (perhaps any school for that matter) cannot be administered on a daily and ongoing basis by staff who are not trained and who do not have the necessary background or information to make important decisions. It took us, as a group of heads of department and school administrators, two years to understand the vagaries of collaborative decision-making and, even now, we sometimes stumble over, and stray from, our agreed-upon terms of reference. None the less, each head of department and the school administrators are intricately linked with their respective organizations in the system or administrative groups beyond school, and have more time to interact with peers and associates as well as to read current policies, procedures and literature. There is a preparedness in this group and a background knowledge that makes them effective in their role.

On the other hand, classteachers have daily responsibilities for the delivery of the curriculum through a course of study. Curriculum and programme issues weigh heavily on their activities and are a major focus of their day-to-day professional life and their work with students. I believe teachers should have more responsibility for that which affects them more directly. Consequently, it seems to me that they should play an important role in leading and directing the school in programme-related issues. Many opportunities have surfaced at the school and we have identified the following as key areas of development:

- General-level programme.

- Gifted programme.
- Race–ethno-cultural issues.
- Computers across the curriculum.
- Co-operative group learning.
- Evaluation of students.

Within each of these areas, the programme planning team has organized committees of interested staff. Each committee set out goals and objectives for itself and designed plans of action. The impact of this has been profound. For example, we are the only school in our jurisdiction (LEA) that has a statement on race and ethno-cultural equity. These efforts, in turn, led directly to the development and implementation of a policy on race and ethno-cultural equity for the Halton Board of Education. We have convened a number of workshops for staff on teaching strategies for the general-level student. We also have a comprehensive plan for the evaluation of students in our school that addresses every issue connected with evaluation, including examination-writing and absenteeism and how these relate to marks.

We really had to wrestle with the line of authority for the programme planning team: if this team were to be successful, it had to have the autonomy to act somewhat independently of administration and heads of department (the cabinet) yet, at the same time, it had to be accountable for its responses and its recommendations. It was decided that a head of department would sit on the team and act as an adviser and communication link between the cabinet and the team. In so doing it was not intended that the head of department would unduly influence the group but rather would provide counsel and advice, while reflecting the opinion of the cabinet when necessary.

In effect, the programme planning team has operated independently of the cabinet and yet it has made decisions consistent with the directions of our school (as expressed in our school growth plan) and with our cabinet (as expressed through our procedures and school policies). It has proved an excellent opportunity for staff to learn and grow as professionals, not only in the specific areas of interest identified above but also through the variety of training and professional-development opportunities we have been able to offer. More staff have been promoted out of this high school over the past five years than any other high school in the region. No doubt this is a tribute to the quality of staff and the commitment they demonstrate to their own professional growth and development. At the same time, the leadership experiences and professional growth fostered through the team has been beneficial.

THE DISTRICT CONTEXT

It would be helpful to know a little more about Halton Board of Education and, more specifically, about the initiatives and efforts it was making at the time school improvement and the school growth plan were being implemented.

By 1987 our board was committed to regenerating the efforts of all schools in its region. The wealth of research evidence coming from school-effectiveness literature led to the development of a school-effectiveness task-force and other initiatives, at both the school and superintendency level. These put the Halton system to the forefront of school improvement in the province of Ontario. In 1988 a new director of education sought to re-organize the system's administrative structure. One of his major aims was to create a superintendent who would be responsible for school-growth planning.

The overriding philosophy behind this effort was that school-based planning was critical to improvements in performance in schools and that resources must be made available in order to accomplish this. It is important to distinguish between school-based management and school-improvement programmes: school-based management implies a broader authority and greater power than that which exists in our system at present. It also implies that the school has complete autonomy over such areas as staffing and budgets, and a greater share of the development of rules and procedures. Although we are moving towards this, in Halton the emphasis is still on school-improvement programmes. The director provided a new approach to our school-improvement programme. School-based planning became important under this re-organization and, subsequently, more resources (both human and financial) were made available to us.

The board continues to place much emphasis on collaboration and developing collaborative relationships among decision-making groups in a school, as well as collaboration between teachers as this relates to the planning and delivery of instruction. A learning consortium emerged from this exercise – a joint, collaborative effort between Halton, the University of Toronto, three other boards of education in the province and the Ontario Institute for Studies in Education. School staff received training in a variety of instructional techniques and, in turn, were expected to return to their schools and provide direction and leadership to other staff. Budgets were established specifically for the support of school initiatives, and White Oaks took ready advantage of this. It provided opportunities to cover teachers' classes with substitutes while the teacher developed new programmes and new instructional techniques. It also enabled us to bring special resource people into the school to work with our staff. It also allowed us to free staff from classroom duties from time to time to visit other projects, schools and initiatives, not only in our region but across the province. The consortium experience was particularly helpful for me because of the presentations I attended: the opportunity to work with my peers was invaluable in the sorting and visualizing that had to take place. The input of authorities from higher education and the research community should also not be underestimated.

THE FUTURE

Our school growth plan is now a one-year plan: the forces acting on secondary schools preclude long-range planning or, at the least in my opinion, make it extremely difficult. As our plan adjusts to these vagaries, I see the need for increased feedback from parents and students as one of the most important alterations we must make. We have already increased the membership of our goals committee to include more parents and students. At the same time, we will continue to focus on the projected rapid growth of our school, and the ever-increasing diversity of our student population. Ontario is also contemplating a considerable redesign of secondary education. The level system is to be replaced, at least in grade 9 and possibly grade 10. Computers and other technology will be a major challenge. One of the three elementary schools that feeds our school has already entered into a contract with a major computer manufacturer and has more computers at every grade level than has ever been seen in this province.

Clearly the challenges are many but so are the opportunities. This school is committed to providing opportunities for staff to grow. Only through a collaborative, decentralized and democratic process can the school begin to meet the needs of our staff, our current students and those yet to come.

Commentary

As the head of the only non-British school to feature in this collection, Leggatt's discussion illustrates both contrasts and similarities with his counterparts on the UK side of the Atlantic. Unlike many other contributors his attempts, when new in post, to introduce change, appear to have been considered by those involved as not only timely but also welcome. Indeed, the continuing 'give and take' of a staff group where consensus is the norm and no vote has ever been needed on any issue, might be a situation deemed little short of idyllic by other contributors.

The introduction of 'semestering' (similar to the UK modular course structure) is undoubtedly easier and more feasible to introduce in a system that, unlike the UK, is not directed towards competitive, norm-based public examinations. The greater flexibility of the system Leggatt describes is exemplified by the scope it offers for the cross-registration of students from the vocational school. Although, in Britain, there are many examples of schools joining local consortia in order to offer students access to a wider range of courses, invariably these courses are of a two-year duration, leading to public examinations.

Other contributors have described their schools' development plan. Leggatt's scheme differs somewhat in the role assigned to the goals committee, in the relatively brief one-year cycle and in the formalized evaluation process employed (including a prize for the 'winning' contributors).

Leggatt is positive about the jurisdiction (local authority) in which his school is located – particularly in terms of support for risk-taking innovations and resources to facilitate them. It is interesting that the Halton School Board has been at the forefront of efforts by school boards to put into practice the lessons learnt from effective schools research, in a more overt fashion than has been the case in the UK.

7
Vivien Cutler
St Paul's Way School

Vivien Cutler graduated from Glasgow University in philosophy and politics. She took a post-graduate certificate in primary education at Jordanhill College of Education and a university diploma in education and psychology. After two years' teaching in primary schools in Glasgow, she was seconded to the Inner London Education Authority (ILEA) course for the teaching of 'slow-learning and difficult children', latterly known as TOCSEN (teaching of children with special needs). She then worked in a variety of comprehensive schools in Wandsworth, Tower Hamlets and Islington, teaching special needs and humanities and holding posts of responsibility as head of department, head of year, in charge of primary–secondary liaison and curriculum co-ordination. In January 1988, after three years as a deputy head, she became head of St Paul's Way School in Tower Hamlets.

THE SCHOOL

The school is at present sixth-form entry but is scheduled to expand to eighth-form entry by 1993, in line with rising rolls within the borough of Tower Hamlets. Located near Docklands and the City, in a landscaped, three-acre site, the school buildings date from 1968 – not the golden age of school architecture. There are two blocks: the main teaching block, which also houses our Hearing Impaired Unit (HIU) in a purpose-equipped suite of rooms, is a six-storey wedge linked to a two-storey block containing the hall/theatre, gymnasia, swimming pool, the design technology, music and drama departments and our pastoral base/dining areas. St Paul's Way is a mixed, county school with no religious affiliation despite its name, which was taken from the road bordering one side. The site is used seven days a week by the community for adult education or by the youth service and voluntary organizations.

Bounding the site are three large, low-rise council estates, two very busy through – routes, and a gasometer. This is inner city writ large. The council estates are polarized: first, largely Bangladeshi; second, largely white with a few Afro-Caribbean; and the third is more mixed. The first estate is the oldest of the three, the most dilapidated and the least likely to exhibit tell-tale signs of 'right-to-buy' home-ownership. A primary school is situated in the estate and we take virtually all their 11-year-olds at transfer. High unemployment is endemic in the area (though many of our male parents are of retirement age) and those in work are less likely to be in skilled or non-manual occupations than in any other inner-London borough. In the vicinity are some pockets of gentrification but, even where these contain couples with children, they are unlikely to send them to St Paul's Way. Pupils come from right across Tower Hamlets and from the neighbouring boroughs of Hackney and Newham, often because of the direct transport links.

Over its twenty-year history the school's intake has shifted, from white working class, to mixed white and Afro-Caribbean, to predominantly Afro-Caribbean, to (within the past seven years) minority to majority Bangladeshi. More recently, we have experienced a prevailing pattern of about 70 per cent Bangladeshi pupils with white and Afro-Caribbean the next most numerous, and smaller, but significant, numbers of Somali, other African (mainly Nigerian), Chinese, Vietnamese, Turkish, Indian, Pakistani and occasional groups of travellers' children.

There are further important characteristics of the intake. Not only is it ethnically diverse but it is also highly mobile. Since September 1987, for example, the number of transactions (i.e. pupils coming on roll or leaving the school as a percentage of the mean number of pupils in any year) has ranged from 40 to 54 per cent. This does not include those (mainly) Bangladeshi students who go for 'family home' holidays ranging from six weeks to anything up to nine months without being taken off roll. Perhaps the most trenchant example of this rate of mobility is the figure of only 23.3 per cent of 1989 year-11 leavers who had spent the full five years of second-ary education at the school without any break. Some eight out of ten pupils do not have English as their first language and, of these, well over half have a level of competence in English (at entry) that does not give them full access to GCSE-level courses. Of the monolingual pupils, over 70 per cent have a reading age two or more years below that of their chronological age.

The final feature of the intake that presents a particular challenge is the considerable gender imbalance. When I arrived at St Paul's Way, there were three or more boys to every girl: the ratio has now 'stabilized' at 1.9:1. Muslim parents are especially keen on single-sex education for their daughters and this militates against balance in a mixed school like St Paul's Way, which attracts a predominantly Muslim male intake.

PERSONAL PHILOSOPHY OF EDUCATION

Perhaps Poincaré and the chaos theorists have more to offer the head of this school in terms of a philosophical framework than those recondite reverends of the nineteenth century so frequently quoted by some educationists. Certainly, any philosophy of education, to be relevant, must be able to accommodate a perpetual state of flux and unplanned occurrences. Teaching largely in multi-ethnic and often disadvantagd, marginalized communities has highlighted for me equity as the cornerstone of such a philosophy. This is not, however, a concept to which our communities subscribe universally, nor interpret similarly, even if some notion of equal opportunities is often articulated. If the locus for the transmission and translation of this belief into action is the school, we immediately face problems. Whether the reasons are socioeconomic, personal or a lack of understanding of the structure and role of the English – or any – education system, attendance at school does not always figure highly in some community perspectives. Despite this, we are fortunate to have the majority of pupils *in situ*. We now must overcome the perception (by parents and occasionally by staff) of the school as an outpost of social services or by pupils as an extended leisure and social centre.

Within this plethora of viewpoints, I have tried from the outset to identify the school as a centre for learning, both academic and social, with a moral dimension that acknowledges that everyone brings his or her own norms but that, to ensure equal access to the process of self-development and to the whole curriculum, some basic tenets will differ from those of their home communities. This is most notable in the area of gender equality but it can also underpin a whole gamut of issues from notions of functional literacy or of achievement and progression to that of the administration of justice. (Try playing Portia to the parent who suggests you dispense justice, without recourse to further investigation of witnesses, by beating to a pulp his or her child, the other child or even the teacher.)

The issues of access to the curriculum, the movement towards autonomous learning and the constant need to heighten expectations – hence creating the conditions for the raising of achievement – are central to equity. With the majority of pupils developing or attaining bilingualism and a significant number with special educational needs, access to the curriculum encompasses far more than good mixed-ability teaching and differentiated learning. Choice of syllabuses, classroom management strategies and methodologies have to take account of up to thirty individuals who may all have language and/or learning needs, whose length of time in the school, or indeed any school, may be minimal and who may be further denied access through gender – this on top of a normal distribution curve of ability level. It is hardly surprising that teachers may find it impossible on occasion to create adequate resources to support each student or to resist a deficit culture model in which the prevailing response is, 'Well, what can you expect from these children?' There is, additionally, the understandable temptation to try to cope with the multiplicity of need as if it were uniform. Thus the relative merits of the in-class support/withdrawal debate becomes ideological rather than focused on individual or group requirements. The exploration of the mixed-economy approach is gaining currency, which is good news for the demise of stereotypes as well as for the quality of learning experience for students.

Equity is a whole-school issue and does not emerge solely through the classroom. The shape of the day, school structure and staffing of the curriculum, the quality and pattern of relationships and of the environment must all offer to each student a positive reflection of his or her worth, initiative and aspirations. The environment is a priority in the agenda of most new heads in inner London. St Paul's Way offers an oasis of green amidst the adjacent estates and so is used as an informal leisure area and cut through by local residents, often out of hours. That it is landscaped and large (by Tower Hamlets' standards) is an undoubted advantage, but its very openness has invited an endless stream of intruders, some of whom have been responsible for acts of vandalism, harassment and violence. The quality of the environment here embodies both the aesthetic and the secure. The male adolescent penchant for battles over territoriality, underpinned by racial tensions, has resulted in skirmishes on the perimeter of the school, which have increasingly featured the use of weapons. We have taken a strong stand to keep this very real aspect of life in the local communities outside the gates of the school. The institution *has* to represent a safe area where there is no place for weapons, where there is no place for disagreement other than through the medium of words. A place for learning can empathize with the tensions caused by external events and it can provide a forum for talking through these schisms (which arise overwhelmingly out of school) and for activities that can channel young people's energies in leisure pursuits other than the spectator sport on offer too frequently at lunchtime and after school recently. (That there are so many marginalized and disempowered groups of young men in the community does little to help.)

We cannot directly affect policy at local or central government level that might impact on our community to improve the overcrowded and drab environment or other aspects of the quality of their lives. What role can we effectively play? We hope we can enable young people to learn to co-exist safely and to explore their common needs and differences in a non-threatening arena. That is the aim. I would not claim we have travelled more than a tiny distance along the road to fulfilment. It is, I trust, not too pious to conjecture that, if we fail, yet another generation will be denied equity.

Rev Edward Thring may not have had the experience of his students being hospitalized as a result of mindless and savage racist attacks on the streets, but he would undoubtedly have subscribed to the concern to improve the appearance of the buildings and grounds. Through financial support from a variety of sources, we have been able to transform external areas from the design briefs of our students, elicited through a school-wide competition. We have also made our reception areas more attractive and welcoming and featured displays of pupils' work more widely. These changes, relatively minor in scale, have focused on the quality of experience for student and community users and increased the feeling of ownership, resulting in a reduced level of vandalism. By improving the environment, girls have been made to feel less marginalized and more inclined to use the site extensively.

How can one translate a philosophy of education based on equity into aims for the school? One way has been to work with a small group of senior and middle managers (on an extended management course) to try to encapsulate the essential nature of the school in a brief written aim. The result was as follows:

> The effective deployment of personnel and resources and the management of the curriculum will enable students to understand and to create coherence out of their dislocated experiences and the variety of expectation of the school and the community, thereby achieving the qualifications and social skills for a successful life beyond school.

This is a statement widely recognizable to all who know the school. We are now in the process of converting it into a policy that can be readily understood by students and parents. Some aspects of this are already in place in our code of conduct, drawn up after widespread consultation with pupils, parents, support and teaching staff and governors. Other aspects have still

to be refined or implemented through our Institutional Development Plan
(IDP) that, supported by relevant in-service activity, will serve as a framework for whole-school initiatives over the next three years.

ORGANIZATION AND MANAGEMENT OF THE SCHOOL

Fortunes have been made writing about the management of change in
schools. The scenario commonly depicted is one in which change is a process
generated either internally, usually by choice, or from without, involuntarily.
In both cases, the process impacts on relative stability. Any institution that is
in itself in a perpetual state of flux in its constituent parts must be enabled to
accommodate yet more change through planned (though flexible) management – or else risk implosion. But it is hard to maintain the consistency of a
philosophy and its systematic implementation when contending with unplanned occurrences (ranging from arson and violence to a situation where
more than a quarter of teaching posts are vacant).

In this context it is easy to assume that St Paul's Way is a phenomenon –
that the degree and rapid nature of change (i.e. destabilization) demand a
unique style and structure of management. This is a hypothesis the senior
management has posed in its more hard-pressed moments. The current
theory (ripe for demolition by whatever next assails us) allows that the
style and structure do withstand most stresses but that there needs to be
greater whole-school responsibility in implementing policies. These cannot
work successfully if practised by a few members of staff only, however
effective. Over the past two years, senior management (the deputies and
myself) has worked closely as a team. I have been fortunate to have been
able to appoint all but one of the team and the formulation of clear job
descriptions has patently fostered an understanding of the parameters of
the roles. I delegate widely to my deputies, not only because the multi-
facetedness of the role makes it impossible to do otherwise given a seven-
day week of a mere 24 hours a day, but also for their professional development – the acquisition of skills through undertaking a broad range of
responsibilities – and their job satisfaction. The idea, although still somewhat inchoate, is for each deputy to rotate responsibilities every couple of
years. Our working day involves considerable time spent in informal discussion: this helps to bond the team and to develop a consistency of approach, which is not the same as uniformity of viewpoint. In addition, we
hold a weekly meeting with a formal agenda as well as a fortnightly one
with the wider management team (senior teachers).

As a school in an authority yet to embark on local management of schools (LMS), it has been possible for all of us to undertake timetabled teaching commitments as well as our (often large) share of cover. There is an abiding dilemma about teaching for a head with such a large part of her role involved in boundary management (both metaphorical and literal at St Paul's Way!) and in the run-up to the implementation of LMS. I have resolved, with considerable regret, not to continue into GCSE with my year-9 class but to teach one year-7 group in a new course. While spending an evening trying to set three or four levels of task for a lesson, I have often relished the space a non-teaching role would afford. However, the advantages of first-hand knowledge of the demands of classteaching at our school and the learning experiences of the pupils far outweigh the minimal gains that might accrue from a less superficial reading of the multitude of DES guidelines. This is not to mention the 'street cred' rating a teaching head gets. Nor do I regard my involvement in curriculum development as indulgent. LMS in a community-orientated site with the extra dimension of a hearing impaired unit will no doubt diminish that role in time, too.

How is it possible for me to gain any overview of what is actually happening with such a high rate of mobility (recently of staff as well as students) and the range of externally generated activities? On the level of pupil experience, I maintain a very visible role round the school, taking the major share of senior duty patrol (a must for repelling intruders as much as for troubleshooting along corridors or in classrooms), daily dinner supervision (about 500 pupils have dinners), taking a number of assemblies and going into lessons to support, encourage and to see the curriculum in action. This high-profile approach is extremely time-consuming and, in a large site, physically demanding. However, it does give the senior management team (SMT) greater insight into both the overt and hidden curriculum than any other method we can conceive of. We share out the heads of department and year among us to enable us to support and supervise the middle managers in delivering their part of the system and in their contribution to whole-school issues.

The difficulty of monitoring and evaluating the implementation of whole-school policies whose existence is so vital for our shifting school population is exacerbated by the time spent on outward-directed activities. Through LEA and inspectorate frameworks, we hope to write into the agenda of each department or pastoral year team a greater role for internal assessment of all aspects of their work. Every generic role (e.g. head of department or form tutor) is published in the annual staff handbook, as well as those of each of the SMT and of the senior teachers. With so many staff having been appointed since I took up post, virtually everyone now has a job description that reflects our priorities: I am gradually updating, with consultation, those of remaining support and teaching staff.

For a teacher new to our school, whether a supply teacher, probationer (of whom we have had sixteen recently) or a head of department, the handbook should provide an indispensable tool for factual information, for description of roles and for statements of policy. There is nothing more frustrating than to plough through acres of worthy prose only to find that practice bears little or no relation to it. To publish nothing – because a policy has not been revised recently or the relevant working party has produced only tentative guidelines – seems to me equally self-defeating. Better to say that a policy statement is emergent and that the handbook statement reflects 'where we're at'.

One major change in the management of the school has been the effect of the Education Reform Act 1988 (ERA) on the role of governors in policy-making. Some staff have found it hard to come to terms with the right of the governing body to make the final decision and to having to direct their opposition to a more amorphous and less readily available group than 'management'. The Act seems to have engendered a new rhetoric for decisions that are taken that do not coincide entirely with staff wishes. The response is often that there has been no or insufficient consultation and that they should have been able to negotiate on the outcome. This muddying of the terms 'consultation' and 'negotiation' can be used effectively to prolong dissent, and I have found it important to re-state that heads are not (to date) empowered to negotiate conditions of service and that consultation can take many forms, ranging from direct voting on an issue where the majority decision is accepted, to the eliciting of views to inform the SMT perspective. Ignore specifying the nature of the procedure at your peril!

The difficulty in accepting governing body or management decisions as final is, in some respects I think, a reflection of the eroded sense of professional worth felt by most teachers reeling from the barrage of 'back-of-envelope' policies and the removal of (real) negotiating rights over pay. The role of the head and that of the governors can become increasingly symbolic and the focus of all discontent.

As an inner-London borough recently transferred from ILEA, Tower Hamlets does not have to implement LMS until 1992. The effects on a school such as ours will undubitably be profound. I hope that the formula eventually submitted to the DES will be sufficiently sophisticated to reflect the cost of the numbers with language- and learning-support needs, the expense of maintaining single-sex groups in certain curricular areas in order to ensure equal opportunities and the fact that, despite present undersubscription in our sixth-form entry, we none the less require a full timetable structure to teach the curriculum while being staffed only on the basis of raw pupil numbers. The on-costs of the mobility rate involve not only an enlarged support staff to deal with the administration but also an above-average use of consumable departmental materials for each new student who arrives and the need to replace those only partially used by any departing students. (As an indicator of the significance of this factor, there has been no week in the last few years in which we have not taken on and/or taken off roll at least two pupils. Annually, we average four to six new pupils each week, balanced by an almost similar number leaving.) High mobility is being considered currently by the borough as one of a range of educational priority index (EPI) factors to complement the age-weighted pupil numbers basic formula.

Community provision on site is extensive: under LMS this is expensive on energy where vast areas of the building are not designed for conservation and there is little possibility of zoning off whole unused parts. Seven-day-a-week usage involves additional wear and tear on existing resources and an increased risk of vandalism, not to mention the extra cleaning hours warranted. To balance the budget, the governors might feel inclined to look at more lucrative returns from the site users and the vital issue of access for the whole community could be at risk, more especially if the strategic role likely to be played by the authority in giving guidelines on community access and charging policy is vitiated by currently espoused government pronouncements on the reduction of the powers of LEAs. Life-long education and leisure provision that is economically accessible to the whole community is surely an integral feature of a policy of equity.

At present, the deployment of resources in our LEA-delegated budget is worked out by SMT in consultation with governors and the monies available for departmental or pastoral use are shared out by a working party using a weighting system (based on the level and cost of consumables) and number of pupil-teaching hours. Special projects or new courses are given set amounts. With the advent of LMS, each manager will need far more than at present, to make decisions on resource allocation with a whole-site perspective. LEA and schools will have to provide quality in-service education and training (INSET) to ensure the knowledge and confidence for this role.

An interesting adjunct to the general debate about the nature of formula funding relates to our school-attached HIU. Taking about twenty pupils, this unit does not qualify as an independent entity entitled to its own delegated budget. Yet it is vital to identify its enhanced level of funding as discrete or the money could find itself submerged in the general pool and vulnerable to any governing body whose priorities did not accord with the needs of these pupils with very special resourcing requirements.

ORGANIZATION AND MANAGEMENT OF LEARNING

Imagine you have just come to London from your home in Bangladesh. You have had some primary schooling there but none at secondary level. You can understand Bengali but can read and write only a little; your home dialect is Sylheti, which has no written counterpart. You are 15 and technically should be entering year 10 to undertake your GCSE courses. As you speak virtually no English, entry into year 10 is fraught with the likelihood of frustration and failure. This challenge – also relatively affecting the newly arrived Kurdish or Filipino secondary-school-educated refugee who is literate in a Roman script – confronts schools such as ours on an almost weekly basis. By putting the student into year 9, he or she is given a greater possibility of access to a curriculum that will eventually lead to qualifications but that can be dispiriting to undertake with the certain knowledge of indifferent grades (or failure) at first attempt. Some young people are more mature than others and it can be as problematic for them to be with students perhaps considerably younger than themselves in every way as to be wrestling with GCSE taught in a foreign language. We are often so preoccupied with the bureaucracy associated with the admission of new pupils that we forget the culture shock they may suffer: different teaching methods, expectations of equal opportunities and cultural diversity. There is an increasing number of young people arriving with refugee status and it is hard to envisage the effects of persecution or being conscripted – and being shot at. The experiences of these students mean that they often require more support than merely access to English and to the full curriculum. Where are the resources to help? Even if our budget could sustain a qualified counsellor, who could effectively deal with traumas brought from places as diverse as Ethiopia and Laos? At an institutional level, we must try to involve all our pupils in the school community and in the learning process.

   It is significant that the numerically largest department in the school is that of English as a second language, which supports pupils in the classroom to gain access to the curriculum and collaborates with colleagues in teaching method and curriculum development. The majority of the department are bilingual (mostly Sylheti/Bengali speaking although other languages are represented as well) and this gives opportunities for greater conceptual understanding through the use of the community language. Bengali is on offer as a major language with French from year 7 and many pupils achieve success at GCSE earlier than year 11 (as do other community language speakers in, for example, Hindi or Urdu).

The present option of choosing syllabuses based predominantly on coursework has undoubtedly been more favourable to our bilingual learners. Apart from the time for re-drafting, terminal examinations can hold even greater terrors for them than for their monolingual peers. Despite years of protestations from teachers in inner-city areas, examination boards still insist on framing questions in sentences laced with inversions, parentheses and complex subordinate clauses. To any child with language or learning needs, this can turn the procedure into an inaccessible nightmare. Of course, an interpreter, dictionary or amanuensis is still unacceptable to most examination boards except where a statement of special educational need exists, although more latitude is now being shown by some boards in the use of community languages in coursework material. Thus many students do not achieve the grades of which they are intellectually capable (the examinations being a test as much of competence in English as that of the subject by the end of year 11). How much more appropriate would be the option of a three-year GCSE – for those who had just entered the country in year 10 or 11 or whose English was still weak – than the existing system of two years and then a one-year GCSE mature examination, often in a post-16 institution.

Considerable success has been achieved by using an individualized mathematics scheme where large numbers are entered for GCSE mathematics from year 9 onwards. At present, we have a policy that allows any student who has completed the coursework, attended regularly and would benefit from the experience, to sit the examination. For how long can this be sustained under LMS? We offer a full range of National Curriculum subjects at key stage 3, with the addition of drama, all taught in mixed-ability groups. Within any core-subject lesson there may be in-class support for those with language and learning needs and for any hearing-impaired pupils. Curriculum mapping and the implementation of the cross-curricular aspects of the National Curriculum are to be welcomed, not just as a means of facilitating inter-departmental co-operation, but also of weaving coherence into what must be a totally fragmented experience for most of our students.

Major problems arise in the area of assessment. (I shall not dwell on the final shape of the curriculum at key stage 4 as this seems to alter daily. Many heads will no doubt wish to allude to the bureaucratic overload and the inappropriateness of many of the forms of assessment proposed.) There are fundamental problems facing teachers in the assessment of pupils who may arrive at any time from year 7 to 11 with few or no records from a previous school. What methods do you use to assess a pupil who has stayed at the school for one or two weeks only or whose total lack of English denies him or her the possibility of being assessed even at level 1 of any attainment target in most subjects? The waiving of the rules is not appropriate for the vast majority of our students where exposure to the whole curriculum with appropriate support will lead eventually to greater linguistic competence with which to express their understanding and skills. There may be some need to consider this procedure for those with pro-found hearing impairment or learning difficulty, but this will only be under-taken with the most thorough discussion and agreement among pupils, parents and staff. What such a procedure will do to our 'performance-indicator rating' when levels of attainment are published is too risible to contemplate. (In fact, when ILEA used to assess the examination results of its schools weighted by a sophisticated set of EPI-type factors, our school was deemed to be performing at an above-average level. The government seems less enamoured of the idea of identifying the context in such a manner.)

I have recently been involved in trialling a key stage 3 standard assess-ment task (KS3 SAT) in English, devised by one of the local consortia bidding for the contract. Although an immensely time-consuming business, and one not entirely enlivened by stimulating materials or tasks, it was a fascinating exercise in coming to terms with how narrow the concept of the 'average child' is – and this was a consortium generally regarded as being more sensitive to the needs of inner-city and bilingual students than most. Briefly, the whole exercise was heavily content driven, almost totally inac-cessible to stage-1 and many stage-2 learners and, in assessment terms, it assumed a level of dispassionate teacher intervention well-nigh impossible in a classroom where so many genuinely require help to be able to progress independently. In addition, I had to rewrite many source materials. The content did recognize the multi-ethnic school but not through the type and level of the tasks. It was extraordinarily frustrating to find descriptions of levels of attainment that did not fit any pupil directly: they might contain elements on any level from 2 to 8, even in the same task! No account was taken of the additional time needed by bilingual pupils, or those with special needs, to complete assignments. I sincerely hope that some notice is taken of the detailed and constructive criticisms advanced by my colleagues and myself on the nature of the standard assessment task. Even the veiled assumption (in relation to presentation of material) that schools were awash with computers or that pupils might have access to word-processing facilities at home showed a lack of realism.

The shape and delivery of the curriculum at St Paul's Way is decided through working-party, middle-management and whole-staff consultation. We have been moving towards an extended core at key stage 4 (KS4) so that all pupils take English, mathematics, science, technology, physical education and personal, social and health education and the majority take a language. The quality of the delivery of language and learning support is, as frequently mentioned, vital to student success at our school. The appointment of a co-ordinator for this area will lead, we hope, to the rationalization of the deployment of relevant staff with effective targeting of specific pupils. We need to evaluate continually our use of section 11 and special educational needs staff within the classroom and to ensure all teachers are exposed to a rolling programme of INSET on language acquisition and learning skills.

This aspect of the learning experience, and that of strategies for mixed-ability teaching and differentiated learning, were at the centre of a recent LEA review led by the senior secondary inspector. The review, involving the chief inspector, the senior inspector for special needs and the principal educational psychologist, was of a dipstick type, visiting the school for two days to observe all aspects of school life and to meet pupils, support and teaching staff, as well as wading through piles of school documentation. In addition, subject inspectors (or those still around at the demise of ILEA) made visits to individual departments on the days preceding the main review.

In retrospect, this was a hilarious event, taking place as it did in the midst of some of the worst of the episodic, violent racial tensions of the year. When certain subject inspectors made their visits, they had to pass through mounted police at the access road; amazingly, all was calm inside the school. The main team's visit was punctuated by a day in which some staff chose to take a limited form of industrial action in protest at a decision I had taken to alter the shape of the school day – for many reasons – to minimize the risk of aggressive intruders during 'the troubles'.

The review process was prefaced by a meeting with the SMT who had drawn up an agenda of their priorities for the school. It was reassuring to find that these coincided with those of the inspectorate (if they hadn't, something would have been sorely amiss, I think). The outcomes from the review are being used to develop a framework for the IDP.

One of my first tasks on taking up headship at St Paul's Way was to deal with the aftermath of an HMI report on a full inspection that had happened some fifteen months previously. Apart from the fact that half the personnel alluded to (including the head) were no longer there to act on any recommendations, there was so much past history as to render the whole exercise irrelevant. The hours consumed in procedures to take it to ILEA members for acceptance was not the best use of a new head's time. Furthermore, despite my general experience of HMI as perceptive and incisive, the particular team seem to have been nonplussed by their experience and to have made mordant comments on some points but to have omitted any mention of other key issues. Individual and small teams of HMI do come into the school on specific subjects, such as the compact scheme (see next section) and also in response to broader issues, such as recent chronic staffing shortages. I am pleased to say that the follow-up to both those visits was available rather earlier, and was thus more useful than that of the inspection report.

As with the management of the school, the organization of learning has to recognize its idiosyncrasies. None the less, it is not the only school whose pupils have language and learning needs or who are highly mobile: it just seems to be at the *end* of a continuum of schools with complex needs. Our students are, for the most part, keen to succeed in gaining skills and qualifications and to carry on with their education. I wish I felt more confident that the DES recognized the existence of such students and supported more substantively the initiatives to enable them to achieve their goals.

RELATIONSHIPS

Visitors to the school, of whom there is a fairly steady stream, frequently remark on the friendliness of teaching and support staff and students. (I wonder if this characteristic is just a manifestation of the apocryphal 'East End' or if it is a necessary survival skill in a school where relationships can be so ephemeral?) We have a large staff in relation to pupil numbers, reflecting the needs of the intake and representing virtually the full age-range and length of service. With the governors, I have tried to ensure that the organizational culture of the school offers equal opportunities, promoting an affirmative action policy on staff appointments. This has resulted in far greater numbers of women and ethnic-minority staff joining us to mirror more closely the composition of the school and to provide role models.

I have referred elsewhere to the situation in 1988–9 when whole areas of the school were covered by supply teachers and some departments run by members of the SMT (a situation that resulted from promotion and growth of pupil numbers, not mass exodus). Many posts elicited only one applicant on advertisement and were not filled until the third attempt. A small nucleus of governors spent literally hundreds of hours interviewing, and the chair probably spent as much time on school business – and on site – as most members of staff. With such large numbers joining us in September 1989, we felt it important to hold a special induction on the first day of term. Probationers all have one afternoon a week throughout the year divided among school-based INSET and that offered by the LEA professional development centre and subject inspectors or advisers. We have used both our staff development tutor and another very experienced teacher to induct, observe and support our vast army of probationers. While it is a delight to have so many new and enthusiastic colleagues (of all ages, too), it has proved only a little less destabilizing than the experience of 1988. I find it hard to believe that I introduced only four new teachers on the first day of the 1990 academic year.

Support staff play a key role: our learning resources department (library and media-resources personnel) are vital for the differentiated resources needed to support learning, and the library, with its wide levels of text and increasing bilingual and community language stock, encourages most pupils to read. The department also makes a significant contribution to INSET and produces a high quality of communications documentation, which has been an asset in marketing the school. Our science and technology technicians are all regarded as individuals and the latter has been central to the development of our hovercraft (making, maintaining and racing) team. As in most institutions, the office staff are the fount of all knowledge, especially about pupils. We are lucky to have a Bangladeshi clerical officer who deals with initial inquiries by Sylheti/Bengali-speaking parents, interprets where necessary at interviews and uses the Bengali word-processor for the bilingual communications to home.

The site is open every day of the week and for four evenings. It is large, open and the buildings seem designed to make supervision a nightmare. Good relations with the school-keeping staff and the head of centre (responsible for the adult education and youth provision) are indispensable. Site management meetings are held regularly and the finer points of the interface between access, security and cleanliness are usually ironed out to everyone's satisfaction. Being seen as Solomon can be flattering, but it can be less than welcome on arrival at 7.30 a.m. to be met by an irate school-keeper who wants to drag you round to see 'the thing' floating in the swimming pool or to mediate in a dispute about the quality of the vacuuming.

Before taking up post, I was able to visit the school weekly to interview about 80 per cent of the staff to ascertain their concerns, professional development needs and aspirations for the school. These initial talks helped to avoid the pitfalls of instant confrontation but, as in any institution, there are always those who have a vested interest in retaining the status quo and resist change to the system and culture vigorously. As new staff are appointed, there is a greater chance that different attitudes and ideas will be considered favourably, particularly if one is fortunate enough to have been able to deliver some tangible improvements through change.

Most of my day seems absorbed with personnel issues of one kind or another: disciplinary matters with pupils, parental discussion, staff worries about personal problems, pay – and other colleagues. There are also the intractable difficulties associated with child protection and staff problems. It is, therefore, a pleasure to be able to get out of the office and to be able to carry out some 'minute management' or praise good work and effort. Relations with community representatives and the police have taken on a higher profile recently and this has been one area for which time for other developments has had to be sacrificed. With the expansion of the school to take a further two-form entry in the next few years and the associated building work, there is now an architectural development team appearing regularly on site – at least providing a more edifying topic of conversation than that of cockroach infestation, which lately featured in discussions with an environmental health team.

St Paul's Way was a pilot school for the east London compact in 1987. The scheme has provided some valuable initiatives in bringing together schools and the commercial sector and has had some impact on raising student aspirations. Our young people have gained in confidence from work-experience placements and the contact with those in occupations unthought of and from well outside their social sphere. We have also developed close contacts with business and industry through involvement with the 'business in the community' initiative and the London Docklands Development Corporation. Schools in areas of relative material deprivation need the financial benefits that accrue from such associations and the contacts that can provide opportunities for students and staff alike. I am not totally uncritical of the nature the relationship sometimes takes (a flying visit by a managing director to acclimatize him – nearly always – to the exotic species on show and to the unrecognizable features of State maintained, comprehensive education in the inner city), but I also accept the value of greater dialogue and knowledge and of the breaking down of stereotypical views on both sides.

Certainly, most students are becoming more aware of the possibility of quality job opportunities on their doorstep when the major office towers of the City and Docklands are clearly visible from the school. (I say 'most' students as it seems as difficult to raise the aspirations and achievements of many white pupils and their parents as it was when I first taught in Tower Hamlets fifteen years ago.) The borough has traditionally suffered from an abysmally low staying-on rate and I have become actively involved in work-ing parties to find ways of encouraging students not just to continue with their education post-16 but also to set their sights beyond taking GCSE at a mature level (i.e. re-sits). Much work needs to be done with both young people and their families in the area of role models and I am looking forward to the results of the current series of initiatives that are giving residential placements to our students in higher-education institutions.

Parental Involvement

A school that has a parent body that is predominantly poor, under-educated, may not speak English and is afraid to come out of the house during the evening has a real challenge as regards getting parents into school for discussion of pupil progress or curriculum initiatives or to see their children perform in our termly concerts (in which large numbers participate). When I started at the school, there had just been a year-10 parents' evening to which, I believe, six people came (it was just after the end of industrial action). In the past year we averaged 50 per cent attend-ance for such evenings and a staggering number turned up to hear us talk about compact, careers and option choices for those going into year 10. The transformation has come about through the investment of time in person-alized invitations and reminders, phone-calls home if reply slips have not appeared, lots of bilingual staff to talk to and the provision of quality refreshments. We also hold most meetings from 4.15 to 6.45 p.m., thus generally overcoming the problem of travelling in the dark. We can, and will, improve on what to many readers will appear a pitiful figure to enthuse over but it will all cost time and money and may fall victim to the battle for resourcing under LMS.

Not surprisingly, we do not have a parent-teacher association: former models are inappropriate and we are still unsure of how best to involve the diverse nature of our parent community. We need desperately to find methods of engaging them in dialogue about supporting their children's education that will be sensitive to cultural or socioeconomic circumstances. Thus it is unreasonable to expect much tangible support for a child's edu-cation from a large family living in bed-and-breakfast accommodation, but that does not mean that we should not inform them of the requirements and discuss alternative solutions. We do attempt to consult parents on a wide range of issues, such as the code of conduct and the shape of the school day. It has taken some time to have been wholeheartedly accepted by some parents – a youngish woman head does not quite fit their idea of the charismatic leader, but that seems a diminishing issue. Still a problem is how to get across the notion that the head cannot deal personally with every incident and has to delegate.

Governors

I have already noted the work put in by some governors in terms of appointments. In common with many inner-city schools, we find it extremely difficult to raise sufficient numbers to stand for office in the first place and then to obtain a quorum for meetings. I can understand the 'meetings fatigue' that set in over two years of numerous appointments and also pupil-exclusion meetings, but how we cope with LMS under such circumstances or find ways to involve parents when their representatives don't turn up is a constant worry.

Staff Development

What time is there left for staff development? Finding myself one of the few senior staff with any recent experience of life beyond this school – let alone Tower Hamlets – when I arrived, I endeavoured to support colleagues in achieving professional development through targeting individuals for courses and making myself available for careers advice, application-form writing tips and mock interviews. I have not been able to give as much time to 'listening' recently as I would have wished, nor spent as much time in the staff-room (though some colleagues have a marvellous knack of bending one's ear more regularly than others). I am endeavouring to see individually every person who has completed his or her first year with us to talk about professional development and any concerns, general or specific. This is not an appraisal exercise, although I personally feel that the sudden quiet from the DES on that front is disappointing. We pioneered an SMT appraisal scheme last year, validated by our inspector. From what I have written concerning the tensions of late, you will not be surprised to learn that most of the targets we set ourselves seem to have vanished at the perimeter fence.

Good relations are pivotal in a school with such a degree of diversity and change. So, too, are markers and ceremonies or celebrations that make us into some kind of identifiable community. The participation rate in occasions such as the London record of achievement or GCSE certificate presentations has shot up. They are formal, but unstuffy, and there's always lots to eat! If I were asked to identify indispensable tools for headship, the coffee percolator and biscuit tin would be right up there with the computer.

PERSONAL REFLECTIONS

Colleagues regale you with stories of heads they have known; they come in a number of categories – effortless and charismatic, eccentric and those who sat in their offices doing the crossword and disappearing to rotary-club meetings or golf on a Friday afternoon. No chance of that, but the role seems to have altered even in the last three years. The talk is no longer of values but of effective delivery and the skills of an updated renaissance polymath have become a prerequisite not a bonus. (I really would prefer to have the time occasionally to read up on matters *educational* than to become an expert on the breeding habits of the cockroach or on some obscure building regulation.) However, I imagine it is probably marginally easier to have come into headship never having experienced the previous mode than to have to suffer role confusion in the transition to the present version.

There certainly must be something about the job other than 'megalomasochism' to keep me going back every day. Perhaps what I value most is the opportunity to work in a large and extremely mixed institution. To build and develop teams of all kinds is stimulating but also testing, especially as we are operating at the interface between professional and community aspirations and in a context of unprecedented upheaval. I also, for the most part, relish the variety of the role: no two days are ever the same and there is endless amusement to be wrought from situations you never expected you could be called upon to deal with. The real challenge is to seize the opportunity for implementing ideas you have evolved over a number of years in teaching. The power to enable extended opportunities to be offered to students and professional development for staff is an exciting, if awesome, one. Of course, when it all falls apart and it suddenly becomes your sole responsibility, that's the down side.

There are a number of changes I would want to make both in the short and longer term, some of which, such as a language policy, I have referred to elsewhere. I do have one fundamental change that I would dearly love to see implemented – that of a coherent community education offer on the site. I cannot comprehend the model ILEA sustained of discrete adult, youth and school provision in areas where the need for an integrated approach was paramount. With that kind of flexibility we might be able to engage all sectors of the community in the activities on offer and begin to increase access.

I acknowledge that what I have presented is an idiosyncratic view of headship. My response to the situation I confronted when taking up the post was undoubtedly shaped by lack of experience and, at that time, appropriate training. The style of management may also reflect callow youth; I cannot imagine any of us running around as we presently do when we are in our 'prime'. We ritualistically discuss time management. However, I recently undertook a week's work experience, shadowing another woman manager. The overwhelming feeling I took away with me was that she derived her authority from her wide experience and knowledge of a role that was quite manifold but was not expected to be an expert on every conceivable aspect of management. That gave her the space to reflect, so coveted by heads. And the one change that would make my job more manageable: no change just for a week. Okay, a day, perhaps?

Commentary

More than any other contributor, Cutler raises issues specific to working with disadvantaged communities in an inner-city area. She questions how best mixed schools can meet the needs of a population that is ethnically and linguistically diverse, highly mobile and that has significantly more males than females. Unlike most of the schools of the other contributors, the rapid turnover of staff exacerbates these difficulties.

Cutler also faces up to the challenge of how to deal with equity in a context where community norms mean that it is neither universally supported nor similarly interpreted, and where the effects of unemployment and racial tensions impinge daily upon the school.

Although committed to the model of a teaching head, Cutler has had to reduce her time in the classroom in order to maintain a high level of visibility – to be seen by large groups of students and by unwelcome intruders.

Most contributors comment on LMS. Cutler raises the related issue of the potential risk for special-needs groups that, not having their own delegated budgets, may be vulnerable to a future governing body with different priorities.

The issue of assessment is also raised by others but, for Cutler, the debate is highlighted by the problems of assessing pupils who may arrive, often from overseas, at any time and at any stage, with few or no previous school records.

8
William Atkinson
Cranford Community School

William Atkinson was born in Jamaica and came to Britain at the age of 7, having had no formal schooling. He trained as a teacher at Portsmouth College of Education and later gained a BEd at North London Polytechnic and an MA at London University. Since his first teaching post, in Hampshire, Atkinson's career has been pursued in the inner city, first in the Inner London Education Authority (ILEA) and then in the outer-London boroughs of Brent and (currently) Hounslow. Cranford Community School is his second headship.

THE SCHOOL

Cranford Community School is a large purpose-built community school situated in Hounslow, serving the communities of Cranford and Southall. As a community school, Cranford is well provided for in terms of accommodation and recreational space. In addition to the extensive playing fields there is a large sports hall with weights room, dance studio and small gymnasium, as well as five squash courts, extended library, youth wing, crèche and bar.

The school caters for some 950 students with a sixth form of 145–150. In addition there are approximately 120 adults following daytime classes/courses. These include women returners and print trainees following employment training courses, and YTS youngsters who come to Cranford for the off-the-job training. There is also a large and flourishing adult provision that operates for seven days a week and includes thousands of sports users

143

drawn from within and beyond the local community. At Cranford, school and community provision is administered by the senior staff and myself. We are accountable to the governing body and have to work within broad policy parameters established by the LEA.

Hounslow is situated on the western fringe of London and includes part of Heathrow Airport. Cranford is located approximately one mile from the airport immediately under one of the flight paths. The school, however, is in a mainly residential area with some light industrial warehousing nearby. The majority of the residents are owner-occupiers with only a relatively small number in council accommodation. Because Hounslow is a tight geographical area with a number of well-regarded secondary schools in close proximity to each other, many of the youngsters from Cranford area attend schools other than Cranford and many pupils come from beyond the immediate area.

Over the last fifteen years or so the ethnic make-up of the area has changed from being predominantly white, lower middle class and upper working class to being ethnically diverse. This trend is reflected in the ethnic make-up of the school, with approximately 62 per cent of the pupils being bilingual; the main languages spoken are Punjabi, Urdu, Hindi, Gujerati and Bengali. The indigenous white students represent about 20 per cent, with approximately 18 per cent made up of other nationalities and ethnic groups.

Cranford is fortunate in that each year it receives a reasonably balanced intake. However, in recent years, as the proportion of Asian pupils has grown so has the proportion of boys. There is now a significant and worrying gender imbalance in the form of a lack of girls, especially in the lower school. This state of affairs is recognized as being undesirable but is proving difficult to turn round.

PERSONAL PHILOSOPHY OF EDUCATION

For many years teachers at Cranford have been working to develop a coherent philosophy that would reflect not only what we are trying to do but also help to point the way forward as the school strives to improve the range and quality of experience available to both pupils and adults. We would contend that, although we are a dynamic institution that is eager to assess critically and evaluate the way it goes about its work, there are nevertheless, some core beliefs that remain constant. These core beliefs underpin much of our daily practice and provide an element of stability during periods of rapid change and stress.

As a school we are constantly being enriched by a wide diversity of cultures and races. We strive to recognize and celebrate this diversity in our work and play. We believe that the experiences our pupils and students bring with them to school represent a positive gain to our community.

I would like to state at this juncture that I am one of those unreconstructed 'idealists' who still believe that schools and the experiences they provide can fundamentally affect, for good or ill, the life chances of pupils. However, I do not go as far as suggesting that schools can compensate for the myriad of disadvantages associated with certain socioeconomic positions in our society.

In my opinion, education is in danger of becoming utilitarian – a means to maintain and, if possible, to enhance our capacity to compete with our trading partners while, at the same time, maintaining a relatively stable social order. The emphasis I can detect is on the acquisition of basic skills for all, with higher-order differential skills being provided for a smaller number who are seen as being the 'engine room' for further economic advancement.

There is a danger that, paradoxically, instead of achieving economic advances, such an élitist approach will lead to lower overall standards. The challenge is to reclaim the wasted potential of the 60–70 per cent of pupils who are deemed to be failures at the end of their fifth year in secondary schools. This instrumental view can be seen at play right across the educational firmament, from primary school to our ancient universities. The call is for applied knowledge, knowledge that is measurable in a practical form, that can be translated into the balance sheets of our visible and invisible exports.

It is important that headteachers and others in positions of leadership respond positively to the challenges posed by present developments within education. In my view there are a number of steps that need to be taken urgently. First, we in schools need to recognize and at least partly accept the charge that in the past the school system as a whole has failed properly to equip students with the necessary range of skills to play a full part in the economic life of the country. It is my contention that many teachers and institutions were unnecessarily antagonistic towards projects aimed at establishing links with industry and business. Often, the only reference made in lessons to economic activity within the country was by way of criticizing the capitalist system, with much attention being paid to the unequal distribution of wealth and opportunities. Social divisions within society were also attributed to the inherent unfairness of the workings of the market-place.

Today, I am pleased to say, the picture is very different: many schools have established mutually beneficial contacts with the business community. The Technical and Vocational Education Initiative (TVEI) is now in every LEA in the country and is generally welcomed by the vast majority of teachers. Schools bid enthusiastically for new projects promoted by the Training Agency. The fears that industry would take over and shape the school curriculum in its own interests have simply not materialized.

Second, we must accept that although standards overall, contrary to popular belief, are not falling and, if anything, rising, there is much that we in schools need to do to improve further the levels of achievement. HMI frequently report that many of our students and teachers have expectations that are too low.

Third, while recognizing the shortcomings of the system, we need to publicize widely our achievements and challenge those commentators who insist on denigrating, at every opportunity, State schools. Informed criticism is necessary and is to be welcomed. However, ill-informed one-sided observations, aimed at creating a climate that will make possible the re-introduction of some variant of the discredited tripartite system, need to be vigorously engaged. We need to display a much higher degree of self-confidence when talking about our teachers and schools.

Fourth, we must reject completely any notions that all we should be aiming for is equipping our students with basic skills. What is called for is a determination to pursue policies that are designed to uplift to the highest possible level the performance and achievement of every student.

There are clear implications here for institutional management and classroom practice. The job of working with young people in urban institutions is both rewarding and challenging. Such is the magnitude of the task that only highly committed, skilled and enthusiastic practitioners will find it possible to meet properly the disparate demands confronting them. Far more than intellectual commitment is required; a high degree of empathy and emotional investment is essential if disappointment and disenchantment is to be avoided. A resilient and optimistic outlook is also advantageous.

It is my firm conviction that schools can intervene positively in the life of students and make a difference for the better. Central to our philosophy at Cranford is the belief that high expectations need to be present in every area of school work. These high expectations need to be translated into day-to-day practices and experiences for both adults and students alike. It is not possible to have high expectations for the pupils while entertaining anything less for the teachers, caretakers, cleaners, librarian, technicians, etc.

The other dimension of the school's philosophy is expressed in the view that pupils have considerable power to deploy for or against learning. The challenge for the institution is to engage them constructively in the learning process. This engagement will be determined partly by the value system that exists within the school and partly by the perceived relevance of the overall enterprise. We do not ignore the extent to which institutions can elicit ritualistic responses from pupils by using threats and other forms of coercion and, accordingly, we strive to provide positive goals for staff and students that are realistic and attainable.

ORGANIZATION AND MANAGEMENT OF THE SCHOOL

As a large complex institution, functioning as an integrated community school open 18 hours per day, Cranford requires a good deal of managing. Clearly running such an enterprise successfully is dependent on organizing and co-ordinating the effort of a large and diverse workforce.

All institutions of any reasonable size will demand that at least some responsibilities be delegated to other members in the organization. In the case of Cranford there is the added problem that the proclaimed aim of the school is to act as an integrated community. Given the potential for the school, adult, sports, and youth centre developing their own separate identities and operational structures, great care has to be taken to ensure that these spheres of operation do not disengage from the centre and go their own ways.

We are in the fortunate position of being fairly well resourced. This level of resourcing has enabled me to deploy the four deputies across the complete range of activities on campus. Thus all deputies carry some responsibility for year teams, faculties, administration and elements of the community.

Middle-Management Structure

Immediately below the deputies are a team of three senior teachers. Together we form the senior management team. The senior management team relies on, and works closely with, the general management council (GMC), which comprises all heads of faculty, heads of learning, youth warden, sports warden, house manager, bursar, head of adult education, teacher-governors, senior teachers, deputies and myself. This reasonably large group is fully representative of all sections of the school.

Although the deputies are responsible for the day-to-day operation of
the activities on the campus, the senior deputy has a key role in the overall
management of the site. He not only manages his own areas of responsibility but also 'trouble shoots' across the full range of our work, as well as
deputizing for me in my absence.

I believe the heads of faculty should be given full scope to plan and
manage their area of work. They play an important part in the selection of
staff in their areas; they organize schemes of work and select appropriate
syllabuses; they order material and equipment necessary for teaching; they
monitor and evaluate teachers across their field of responsibility; and they
undertake staff development and prepare reports for governors, parents
and the LEA.

Each faculty is given a budget each year derived from a formula that
takes into account the number of pupils and periods taught. Some recognition is also given to the fact that the cost of teaching material varies
between faculty areas. It is generally understood that practical subjects are
more expensive than other classroom subjects. However, the introduction
of the National Curriculum is undermining this principle.

At Cranford my intention is to be as rigorous as possible in the selection
of heads of faculty but, once appointed, to give them the maximum space in
which to operate. They are left in no doubt they are accountable to me for
all aspects of their work. The deputy heads' role is not only to monitor the
work of the faculty but also to help the faculty to improve performance in
its area.

Forward Planning and Curriculum Development

Over recent years a good deal of our time and energy has gone into responding professionally to the welter of initiatives that have originated
outside the school. The pace of these developments has forced us, at times,
to be re-active rather than pro-active. However, at the same time we have
been grappling with the introduction of the GCSE, the National Curriculum, local management of schools (LMS) and records of achievement, we
have managed to find some time to address a number of school-inspired
developments.

The main vehicle for reviewing and evaluating current practice has been
working parties, operating to specific terms of reference, making recommendations to the GMC of the school. All important issues eventually find
their way in one form or another onto a GMC agenda. From there items
are usually discussed in year teams and faculty teams before a final decision

is taken. In this way, through year teams, faculty teams, GMC and senior staff, every member of staff has an opportunity to contribute to developments within the school.

The main forum for dealing with specific community issues is the community council, which comprises representatives drawn from every affiliated group on site. This body is supported by an executive group. Four members of the governing body are also members of the community council as well as two members of the teaching staff. The community council and its sub-groups, as presently constituted, function as sub-committees of the governing body.

The advent of LMS and changes in the way community activities are funded by the LEA have forced us to rethink fundamentally our priorities for community education at Cranford. Among the concerns we have is a feeling that we ought to be striking a better balance between community use and community development. There are also concerns that our user groups are not fully representative of the local community. The concern has also been voiced by some groups that the available provision is rather too traditional and unenterprising.

These and other issues will feature strongly in the school's institutional development plan (IDP). We hope that the Cranford IDP will allow us to plan more systematically across the campus while, at the same time, ensure that initiatives conform to agreed principles and policy arrived at through consultation.

We believe our existing methods of assessing and evaluating our work will fit neatly into the overall structure of the IDP, providing both for school and the LEA important data on our functioning. It is envisaged that carefully constructed performance indicators will be *one* way of commenting on the effectiveness of our work across a wide area. At the same time, we are fearful that these indicators, if we are not careful, could become an end in themselves and, in the process, distort and misrepresent our achievement. The same is true about 'open enrolment'. There is a danger that we will be pressed to divert scarce resources away from productive areas (i.e. teaching) to non-productive areas (i.e. marketing). To meet this challenge schools must engage and involve local communities in what is going on within their boundaries.

The Education Reform Act 1988 (ERA)

Although I have a number of reservations about some of the developments being brought about by ERA, I take the view that, provided the school is clear about its purpose and enjoys the support of the local population, it will be possible to use creatively the legislation to bolster much of our established practice. I am convinced that local people and teachers have a much firmer grasp of the kind of experience our youngsters need for life than government officials who have little or no experience of urban State schools. The task is to convince community members of the value of the school's activities and programmes of work. Local people will fight for services they value and care for, especially where these services cater for the old, the vulnerable and the young. Local people must feel a sense of shared ownership and mission. Only then can the institution stand up to any unreasonable demands emanating from the centre.

ERA, designed as it was to reduce the influence of local councils, also has the potential to loosen the ties with central government. This opportunity exists. What is called for in a school like Cranford is both vision and enterprise.

Local Management of Schools (LMS)

In the few short months since we received our delegated budget, LMS has proved something of a mixed blessing. Under the LEA formula we are net losers by some £85,000. This is after already removing (over the last two years) approximately £200,000 in teaching-staff salaries. The net result of these existing cuts are significantly increased class sizes as well as increased staff loading. During this period of retrenchment we made a conscious decision to protect the range and quality of non-teaching support (i.e. technician, clerical, etc.). This decision has allowed the teachers to devote more of their time to teaching and less to doing clerical tasks.

On the positive side, we are able to establish priorities and attach resources to them on a scale not possible before LMS. At Cranford we have decided we must bring down class sizes in the lower school while retaining current levels of technical and clerical support. It has also been decided that more resources need to be allocated to fund supply cover to minimize the occasions when staff will be asked to fill in for absent colleagues. I take the view that every effort needs to be made to safeguard teachers' planning and preparation time. Increasingly, I am finding that teachers are having to take home more and more work just to stand still. This cannot be in the overall interest of either staff or students.

These small but important improvements have to be paid for from savings to be located elsewhere in our budget. To this end we have found that, by putting out to competitive tendering the bulk of our minor works and maintenance contracts, we are able to make significant savings. We are finding that contractors increasingly appreciate that they are in a competitive market and price their services accordingly. These contractors are proving most responsive and sensitive to our needs in their bid to capture a share of this new market.

The 'downside' of dealing directly with contractors is the time that needs to be devoted to drawing up full specifications, inviting contractors to bid for the work, consulting with would-be bidders and finally appointing a consultant engineer or surveyor to ensure that the specification is properly met and work completed to a satisfactory level. This time has to be quantified and seen as a cost to be set alongside the final price of the contract.

It is hoped that, in the near future, as we become more adept at writing specifications and inviting tenders, the whole process will become less time-consuming and cumbersome. On balance we are convinced that, in time, LMS will be seen as a beneficial development that will aid our overall management of the institution.

Community Resourcing

The separation of the school budget from the community budget is proving highly problematic in a school that has tried for sixteen years to dismantle, wherever possible, barriers between different areas of its work. So far the LEA has been unable to produce acceptable means of identifying separate cost centres. The situation is further complicated by the fact that a great deal of community education takes place during the day when school classes are taking place.

A number of working groups have met recently in an effort to unravel this and other seemingly intractable problems relating to the cost of providing community education at present levels of provision. After four months of the financial year the governors still did not know what the community budget was to be, or how many of the staff would be met from the school budget and how many from the yet-to-be-determined community budget. The other outstanding areas of concern include caretaking, building maintenance, grounds maintenance and cleaning.

Although Cranford is well placed as a purpose-built community school to exploit its facilities, the same is not necessarily true of a number of other schools who view the advent of LMS as a wonderful opportunity to increase income by making better and more extensive use of their facilities. Schools should take care to calculate fully the true cost of their lettings. Only after they have taken account of energy costs, caretaking costs, cleaning costs and other relevant personnel costs can they think of making a profit. Once this calculation is made, for many schools the financial benefits will be marginal or even negative.

ORGANIZATION AND MANAGEMENT OF LEARNING

The organization and management of learning at Cranford is the responsibility of teams of teachers working in ten faculty areas. Faculties are responsible for deciding upon appropriate syllabuses and schemes of work, purchasing and deploying resources and materials, selecting appropriate teaching styles, deploying teachers to classes and substantially writing faculty timetables. The role of the faculty in inducting and supporting probationary teachers is one that is becoming increasingly important and developed.

Recently there have been wide-ranging discussions about whether we should retain the mixed-ability teaching groups that are currently practised in 80 per cent of the classes in years 1–5. Our mixed-ability approach extends to statemented pupils, bilingual pupils and those with special needs. These pupils, in the main, receive in-class support across the curriculum with some limited withdrawal for intense individual or group work. We believe that the needs of these pupils are best met in the context of doing 'real' work with their peers. Although there is a learning development faculty we take the view that all teachers are teachers of special needs and to this end a number of whole-school INSET days have been provided.

Our approach to mixed-ability teaching is premised on the belief that pupils themselves can be effective 'teachers' given the right environment and encouragement. At Cranford collaborative investigation-based strategies for learning are essential pillars to this approach. An example of this approach in science would consist of an open-ended problem-solving brief, such as 'design a bridge with a given span to support a given mass in the middle'. Students would be required to organize themselves into groups of roughly equal size to discuss the brief and plan an approach. The groups' suggested solutions would then be referred to the teacher to ensure that they were safe to undertake. The next stage would require the groups to work out the apparatus needed and the best way of organizing it. Once the apparatus has been assembled and positioned, groups would attempt to find solutions, derived from the original brief, refining and modifying the approach as the work progressed. The onus throughout is on members of the group working as a team, taking responsibility, sharing ideas and making decisions.

National Curriculum Subjects

At first sight the National Curriculum programmes of study in science, mathematics, English and technology do not pose an immediate threat to our preferred mode of operation. Faculties have had to spend a great deal of work comparing the new programmes of study with our existing schemes of work to assess the extent to which substantial redrafting needs to be undertaken. Fortunately for us, as far as the four subjects that will be on stream in 1990 are concerned, the gaps between what we are doing currently and what needs to be done to meet the requirements of the National Curriculum are not too dramatic.

Although there is a good measure of correspondence between current and future activity as far as subject content is concerned, the same cannot be said for the way we may organize and manage learning in the future.

Undoubtedly we will need to review and modify our faculty system to take on board cross-curricular issues, as well as aspects of the new programmes of study that appear to have been transferred from one traditional area to another. To avoid getting ourselves into a situation where every eighteen months or so we need to change radically our structure in response to further developments of the National Curriculum, we have decided (in the short term) simply to establish cross-curricular working teams and monitor and co-ordinate the delivery of the attainment targets across the curriculum. This whole structure will be overseen by a National Curriculum delivery team. We are conscious that in situations characterized by rapid change, every reasonable effort should be made to provide as much stability as circumstances allow. This is not a 'head-in-the-sand' approach but, rather, a pragmatic view that individuals and institutions can only take so much upheaval before they fall into crisis and become destabilized and demoralized.

The most worrying aspect of the National Curriculum and associated testing requirements is not what we know, but, rather, what we don't know! Reports concerning the trials of standard assessment tasks in selected primary schools only feed existing disquiet in this area. Further, reported comments by ministers about the ultimate scope of the National Curriculum and uncertainty about key stage 4 make it difficult to know what precisely to plan for in our IDP.

RELATIONSHIPS

It is universally acknowledged that teachers are the most important resource within any school. Therefore the well-being and morale of this group must assume a very high priority in any school. Teachers who are well motivated and valued are inclined to be more effective and harder working than teachers who have low morale and low self-esteem.

Heads are keen to make the best use of the diverse talents of their teachers and, accordingly, establish structures that will afford them the opportunity to make a contribution to the running and development of their institutions. For some heads this is a question of enlightened self-interest. However, for others, full staff involvement is an absolute pre-requisite to producing an ethos and atmosphere that is conducive to promoting learning.

At Cranford we are also striving to find ways of involving colleagues in the running and management of the school. One area where we have been able to be responsive to the needs of our teachers is in the area of staff development. By using a methodology that systematically collects information about an individual, as well as faculty needs, we have, over the last five or six years, produced a staff development policy that has enabled the school to introduce and embed an impressive number of curricular innovations. One unintended consequence of this policy has been a significant increase in the number of teachers securing promotion elsewhere, with the result that the intended benefits for the institution have sometimes failed to materialize. This is in many ways a pity but, nevertheless, I still think the policy can be justified both in terms of the school and the benefits it draws from dedicated and enthusiastic teachers, and in terms of the general gain to the education service. We are, after all, recruiting well-qualified teachers who have had their skills enhanced in other schools.

Another area of our work that has recently come under close scrutiny is the school's support for probationary teachers. It is becoming increasingly clear that in the recent past our actions have not lived up to our intentions, with the result that some teachers have had a more difficult start at Cranford than was necessary. Our new programme for these teachers will provide practical help and support within faculties, within year teams as well as from the professional tutor and the deputy head with responsibility for staff development.

Every probationary teacher will have a named mentor in the faculty who, with the assistance of the head of faculty, will be a focus for advice and support, especially with regard to what happens in the classroom. In addition, each probationer will be entitled to be observed on a structured basis, by the mentor, head of faculty, professional tutor and deputy heads.

Within the year teams the head of learning for the year in which the probationer is placed will act as the mentor. This has been identified as an important area many new teachers feel under-prepared for by the Post-

Graduate Certificate in Education courses. Throughout the programme space has been allocated to allow these teachers to raise their own concerns as well as comment on the value of the support and advice given.

Personnel Issues

The imposition of the Teacher Pay and Conditions Act 1987 coloured and continues to colour personnel issues in schools. ERA, introduced with little or no consultation with the profession, has also greatly increased the obligations of teachers at all levels. The fact that the details of ERA are only now being worked out, only serves to exacerbate the situation. Regrettably, the high levels of rhetoric from government spokespersons have not been matched by a realistic appraisal of what is required on the ground to bring about the hoped-for improvements in standards outlined in the various ministerial speeches. Even now, at the time of writing, the Secretary of State is maintaining that the acute shortage of specialist teachers is a minor problem, largely regional and no worse than in other professions.

What needs to be grasped by ministers and the DES is that it is not sufficient just to 'throw words' at a problem. A mixture of exhortation and good intention, of itself, will not lead to improved standards unless it is accompanied by a fair level of remuneration, decent resources in the classroom, reasonable buildings in which to work and some mechanism to allow the profession to contribute to overall growth and developments of the service.

In my view, the time is fast approaching when headteachers will have to decide whether or not their pupils' interests would not be better served by them selectively disregarding some of the more unhelpful strictures from the centre. We cannot go on forever pretending that, at the end of the day, everything can, more or less, be done. The situation demands that headteachers take real responsibility and abandon the role of 'conduit' and say 'no, minister'.

The teachers in my school, at every level, work well beyond their contracted hours, not because they are forced to but because, as first-rate professionals, they see a job that needs doing and do it. It is because of my admiration for the professionalism and commitment of these teachers that I now assume the role of gate-keeper and regulate the flow of extra responsibilities and duties intended to impact on them from whatever quarter. In this matter I am not in any way motivated by a sense of altruism, but rather by a knowledge of what is fair and reasonable.

Pupils

In common with all other schools, we at Cranford recognize that pupils and parents can make a most valuable contribution to the life of a school. The difficulty has been devising appropriate mechanisms to encourage and facilitate their involvement.

The traditional route for pupil involvement has been through year and school councils of one sort or another. These councils provide a useful opportunity for students to organize themselves and articulate the views of their peers over a wide range of topics. However, students can sometimes lose patience with these embryonic democratic structures because of the restrictions placed on the matters they are allowed to discuss. Often they are prevented from discussing and making recommendations on the very issues on which they feel most passionate. Examples here would be teaching staff and the curriculum. At Cranford we have sought to identify a range of issues on which the student councils are allowed to have a full voice. These have included uniform, school meals, use of the building at lunchtime, code of conduct, activities within social areas and year charities. Students are also represented on the governing body as observers.

Teaching Styles

At Cranford we try to convey to students that they have a responsibility for their own learning. This is reinforced by our preferred teaching styles, by the way classrooms are organized and by regular self-assessment by students. The advent of records of achievement has given a further boost to this approach.

Using their records, students are asked, at regular intervals, to comment on their own progress in the different subject areas, as well as on the teachers' comments. At the end of these sessions we usually find that the vast majority of pupils are not only realistic about their work and progress but also extremely hard on themselves when they come to the section that deals with future behaviour. There is sometimes the suspicion that a few students decide to tell us what they feel we would like them to say. However, in general, the students value the exercise and take it very seriously. We are now contemplating how we can build students' comments into our regular review of the content and methodology of the courses.

Extra-Curricular Activities

Students at Cranford are fortunate in the quality and range of extra-curricular activities available to them. The existence of a youth wing on site, staffed by two fully qualified persons and a large group of volunteers catering for school members as well as community members, is a major focus of interest to students. The youth warden and his staff organize year clubs, interest clubs, the Duke of Edinburgh Award, social camping and various off-site activities.

Every effort is made to link the activities of the youth wing to the curriculum in the rest of the school. This is mainly achieved through the pastoral curriculum. Records of achievement offer the opportunity to recognize further the many achievements in this area. The sports-hall staff also contribute significantly to the range and quality of extra-curricular activities, especially during the holidays.

Parental Involvement

Parent involvement can prove just as problematic as student involvement. The Education Act 1986 was designed principally to empower parents and the community in the governance of schools. However, the challenge of getting sufficient parents into school on a regular and frequent basis is proving difficult to overcome. For some schools in some areas there isn't a problem. For schools like ours, which serves a disparate population area where most of the parents are drawn from cultures that are not English or European, the problem can be acute. In recent years a great deal of thought has gone into overcoming the hurdles to parental participation in this and other systems.

At Cranford every student joining us in September is given an individual appointment to meet me with his or her parent/guardian during the summer term. For this meeting students are asked to bring along a piece of work they are particularly proud of. Our initial discussion is centred around this item. From there we move on to consider their motivation for selecting Cranford and to a description by me of what we are endeavouring to do at Cranford. The final part of the interview involves the parent/guardian in outlining hopes and aspirations for their son or daughter's education. The feedback from headteachers in our local primaries is that this meeting is enjoyed by parents and students alike and helps to bridge the gap at transfer time between the two phases. For me, it is important that new parents should meet with me, and that the meeting should be positive and, I hope, set the tone for the future.

The year and school parent–teacher associations build on these early foundations. In September 1990 we introduced a parent advisory group made up of four parents from each year. This group is timetabled to meet once a term to discuss issues of substance that arise out of the work of the school.

At Cranford we take the view that parental involvement is far too precious to be squandered on fund-raising. Instead, parents are invited to take part in a wide range of activities aimed at informing and deepening their understanding of the work of the school. We are keen for our parents to be informed critics of our practice and so assist us in becoming a better place for students and adults alike.

During the Eighties, Cranford has invested a great deal of time and energy in developing meaningful links with the wider community. Our achievements in this area can be seen in the number of external awards that Cranford has received over this period: two curriculum awards in 1984 and 1990; numerous RSA industry recognition certificates; the Science and Technology Regional Organization National Award (SATRO) in 1990, for work with industry; and the Training Agency Flexible Learning Project in 1990.

The school's work with adults, under the aegis of the Cranford Training Group, includes courses in office procedures and management for women returners; industry-orientated language courses; and a range of adult-education classes, from assertiveness to Indian fashion. These courses are well used by local employers, including Heathrow Airport Ltd, British Airways, ICL, Courage and Lyons-Tetley.

PERSONAL REFLECTIONS

In recent years the role of the head has undergone considerable change. In 1984 Hargreaves, in *Improving Secondary Schools* (in ILEA), wrote:

> The pressures, anxieties and frustrations felt by teachers are felt even more by headteachers whose responsibilities for the running of the schools have become increasingly taxing, onerous and complex. Many headteachers are concerned about what they believe to be a steady erosion of their position and authority during the past decade which has made the discharge of their responsibilities even more difficult.

If the headteachers surveyed thought the conditions within which they were working in 1984 taxing, I wonder what they would make of the world we now inhabit. In the last five years the educational landscape has undergone a radical transformation that has brought about fundamental and lasting changes in the way schools are managed. What has not changed, however, is the power schools have to improve the life chances of students. In my view, an absolute priority for the service now is a prolonged period of stability to allow the consolidation of the many recent initiatives. Serious consideration also needs to be given to reducing the demands that are currently being made on schools.

I am firmly of the opinion that headteachers, as a group, must become organized, informed and professional advocates for education. We must abandon our traditional role that encourages us to focus only on our own institutions and accept almost uncritically the prevailing status quo. I believe headteachers must, in a responsible manner, wage a campaign to increase the general awareness and appreciation among the public of what is actually going on in schools. We need to work with parents, governors and other interested parties to press for proper levels of resourcing for education and, in return, accept direct accountability to the local community.

One of the reasons I remain a head and continue to derive much pleasure and satisfaction from my work is the level of support and encouragement I receive from our parents. Our parents place a high value on education and trust the school not to betray their youngsters. My first loyalty is not to the governors, LEA or DES, but to the students and parents. For me they are the most significant groups to whom I am accountable.

Another source of satisfaction for me is the manner in which Cranford's teachers approach and discharge their responsibilities to our students. Colleagues at Cranford have a highly developed sense of justice and fair play and this is reflected in their work with both parents and pupils. Their high levels of commitment remain a constant source of inspiration to me.

Commentary

In reflecting on headship, Atkinson considers the current national context of education. He voices disquiet about low expectations, low achievement and low staying-on rates. Readily acknowledging that schools are not without their shortcomings, he regrets what he sees as the current climate in which public education is so often denigrated. Atkinson (who arrived in

Britain aged 7 with no formal schooling) believes schools can make a different to pupils' life chances and he asks how high expectations for everybody can be translated into day-to-day practices and experiences.

Like other contributors, Atkinson believes teachers are the most important resource within a school. Involving staff in the running and management of the school and establishing an effective staff development policy raises the issue, however, of staff losses – staff moving on to secure promotion and thereby enabling other institutions to benefit from their enhanced skills. Atkinson takes a generous view that the education service, in general, benefits and that, in turn, he recruits staff whose skills have been developed elsewhere.

The issue of how to ensure that headteachers have adequate resources with which to implement ERA concerns him. In his view, heads need to protect teachers from what seem to be unreasonable demands. He also argues for the need for a national awareness-raising campaign to publicize the achievements of schools.

9
Peter Mortimore
Jo Mortimore
Issues in Secondary Headship

The contributors to this book lead very different schools – the only constant feature is that they are all comprehensive, providing for students of the secondary age-group. The schools range from a fairly recently created, diocesan-wide Church of England school, to purpose-built community schools or colleges and are in such diverse locations as the rural Cumbrian border country or the multiracial, inner city. For most contributors, their current post is their first headship. The expected challenges of that novel experience have been compounded by (in some cases) the teachers' widespread action of the late 1980s and (for them all) the momentous changes wrought by the Education Reform Act 1988 (ERA).

As their schools differ, so do their routes to headship. Some, like Atkinson and Collings, demonstrate a steady progression up the career ladder. Alston had a period away from teaching (at the Bristol Resources for Learning Centre) before returning to the classroom. Rao arrived in Britain almost a quarter of a century ago 'with a teaching voucher and a head full of dreams' and went on to become the first Asian headteacher in one of the largest urban LEAs in Britain. Her brief spell in industry, however, proved invaluable. For Flecknoe, voluntary youth work while working for a chemical company provided his route into teaching.

This variation in schools, and in the background of headteachers, reflects the reality of our education service. Traditionally, headteachers emerged from the ranks of teachers having made the transition from school to higher education and back again with little experience of the outside world. Today, additional experience of other jobs is seen as an advantage.

PERSONAL PHILOSOPHY

These headteachers admit to a host of influences on their personal philosophies of education. Alston's somewhat iconoclastic contention that 'deep down I don't believe in schools at all', and his view that 'inflexible' institutions are not the ideal environment for the variety of ways in which people learn, resonates with Flecknoe's view of the importance of the 'village environment' and his assertion that 'systems fail and relationships are precious'. Both these contributors comment on how, when older pupils or adults are asked to recall their memories of school, 'daily lives in classrooms' or 'sitting at desks' is rarely reported. Both Evans and Collings stress the influence on their philosophy of their own personal and career experiences, over many years and, with Alston, emphasize their belief in 'life-long learning'. Although Evans's 'vision' has been developing since his college days, in taking on his current headship of a diocesan school he was, in his words, 'appointed to a philosophy'.

We believe personal educational philosophy to be important – especially at such a time of change. Those heads who are secure in the value of their philosophy are likely to be better able to cope with new demands without (in their attempts to accommodate them) sacrificing their principles. The introduction of 'the market' as the main mechanism for producing quality schooling might induce some headteachers to compete for pupils with their neighbours in an overly aggressive manner, relying on promotional skills rather than the genuine achievement of quality. This is not to say that heads should not compete but merely that the basis of the competition should be the effectiveness of the school. A sound and well-thought-out philosophy, which gives value to educational goals and, in Evans's case, to Christian religious values, may ensure this is the case. Yet personal philosophies cannot be taught. As is evident from these contributions, they develop from personal history and the experience of the examples of others. Modelling is a powerful influence in the education process: each of these heads is now a model for their own staff and the next generation.

EQUAL OPPORTUNITIES FOR PUPILS

Several writers stress the importance they attach to meeting students' entitlement to equal opportunities and to promoting achievement. Leggatt takes pride in the fact that not only is his school, as yet, the only one in the authority to have a policy on race and equity, but that staff efforts have influenced policy development at school-board level. The effect schools can have on students' life chances is particularly noted by Atkinson and Evans and is evident in the statement of philosophy of Leggatt's school. This view has been strengthened, over the last fifteen or so years, by the emergence of the research findings on school effectiveness. Studies carried out in England and the USA have demonstrated that – regardless of the characteristics of pupils when they enter – some schools are able to foster progress in both academic achievement and in positive social development. Given the competitive nature of the entrance to British higher education and, in turn, its potential contribution to life chances, an individual school can make a considerable difference. For Evans this means taking account of (but not being dominated by) negative factors affecting the motivation of inner-city pupils. He refuses to allow counselling to 'compensate for good curriculum and teaching'. This is not to deny the place of pastoral care for, as he admits, 'good schools are like good parents: demanding and caring'. Though as many parents will recognize, it is sometimes difficult to reconcile these twin approaches.

Collings' commitment to educational provision geared towards success for *all* students and her notions of entitlement and equity are echoed by Rao's aim for 'an all-round education for *all* pupils'. Cutler, too, sees equity as 'the cornerstone' of her philosophy. Are these three heads committed to an outmoded concept? While some would argue yes, our view is that there should be no conflict between 'quality' and 'equality'. Both are of the utmost importance. We believe, rather, that to secure quality for a few at the expense of the many is the outmoded concept. It is too easy to create feelings of complacency among a minority and feelings of inadequacy among the corresponding majority. Moreover, as Atkinson argues, such an élitist approach will lead to lower overall standards. Given modern views of intelligence – that it is more multi-faceted and less fixed than was previously thought to be the case – selection of a minority is anyway likely to be very unreliable. The commitment, therefore, of these heads to equity appears to us to be both right and proper.

The potential or actual mismatch between the philosophy of equity and the views of some teachers and parents is an issue both Rao and Cutler have had to face in their multicultural schools. Rao has fought hard to overcome the attitudes of 'housework before homework' of some Muslim parents towards their daughters' studies, while Cutler challenges vigorously the 'teacher-as-social-worker' view of schooling.

Most contributors believe, in Atkinson's words, in 'celebrating the diversity' of the different ethnic groups among students while Alston, through an exchange scheme with a school in Tanzania and his own school in Cumbria, ensures that pupils develop, at first hand, knowledge and experience of another race and culture. Alston comments wryly that 'difficult adolescent boys whom I know dislike, on principle, people from the next small town respect the way the Tanzanians played football, and actually found they liked them'. Interestingly, it is the school least likely to have pupils from minority ethnic families that has put in place this exchange. Other schools can rely on their catchment areas for a diversity of cultural and ethnic backgrounds. Whether planned or not, it is important in a society with as many cultures as Britain that pupils have an opportunity to get to know peers from different backgrounds. This is yet another task for headteachers but is the one the success of which will have profound implications for the future of our society.

THE EDUCATION REFORM ACT 1988 (ERA)

ERA has presented headteachers with both opportunities and headaches. Local management of schools (LMS) has forced a rethink of priorities, given scope for flexibility, but absorbed an inordinate amount of time. Alston warns of the dangers of pre-occupation with finances and marketing: 'unless the product is good the hardest sell in the world won't work'. The financial arrangements under LMS also pose difficulties and, in some cases, may threaten existing procedures and provision (Atkinson, Collings, Cutler). Those heads whose schools are open to the community voice particular fears for the future of what they consider invaluable resources and opportunities. Collings views community education as an ' "umbrella" that shelters pastoral care, support for learning, equal opportunities and education for a pluralist society'. For Alston, the school provides a valuable resource for life-long learning for the local community.

The regular daytime and evening use of the premises (in some cases six or seven days a week) may be a valuable and valued asset, but it can provide extra headaches and demands on hard-pressed staff. As Cutler admits, 'supervision can be a nightmare'. Although Flecknoe considers the senior citizens users 'a bit rowdy', he welcomes the fact that they are 'full of fun and add to the village atmosphere'.

For Cutler, LMS has created anxiety that the related formula funding will fail to recognize the special features and specific challenges (i.e. high student and staff mobility) faced by the school. In Evans's view, LMS has been the cause of *the* main change in his role as head, forcing him to delegate more. It is, of course, too early to evaluate the impact of this particular change and of whether – coupled with the effects of opting out – it will lead to the demise of the LEA as at least one of these heads predicts (and welcomes). Established headteachers are likely to miss the security of having an LEA to take care of the financial and staffing aspects of their schools. Newer heads are more likely to welcome the freedom to use resources as they wish, although few will value LMS if it is accompanied by a reduction in money or teachers.

GOVERNORS

The increased powers given to governors should, in theory, make their nomination or election a matter of serious consideration. While for many schools this is the case, in others it is not possible. In multicultural communities governors are needed who can bridge the divide between a largely white staff and ethnic-minority students and parents. Yet Atkinson, Collings, Cutler and Flecknoe all have great difficulty in recruiting them. Whether this is because the message that such people are needed has not yet got through or whether members of black and minority communities do not feel comfortable working on bodies that are predominantly made up of white people, is not known. It is a pity that governing bodies do not yet reflect the communities they serve, just as it is a pity teachers are mostly recruited from the white majority. Heads would be better supported if there was a greater balance between the ethnicity and culture of their pupil bodies and the adults associated with the school.

NATIONAL CURRICULUM

These heads appear to have responded remarkably positively to the National Curriculum – accommodating it, in Flecknoe's case, into the three-period day and claiming that it can help schools to help students achieve. But there are also criticisms: concern is expressed over standard assessment tasks (SATs) and over their potential impact on impressionable young learners. Collings is determined to maintain the existing work in the expressive arts, while Evans sees the National Curriculum as only the 'minimum entitlement'. Again, it is as yet early days. Until the full details of SATs are stipulated and heads are able to consider the advantages and disadvantages of what have become known as the 'non-statutory' SATs in the foundation subjects, as well as their statutory counterparts in English, mathematics and science, it will not be possible to predict with any certainty the effects they will have on pupils or on schools. Perhaps because of the interest in the novel SATs, these heads comment only rarely on the other main vehicle of assessment, the GCSE.

CHALLENGES TO LEADERSHIP

Not surprisingly, most of the other challenges encountered by these heads were to do with internal matters, such as managing change or gaining acceptance by staff. Leggatt has been fortunate in taking on a school where all concerned seemed ready not only to face but also to welcome change. Others found, however, that misunderstandings over motives can occur. Thus Alston's presence at the school gate, intended to demonstrate a friendly welcome by the new head, was interpreted by staff as a 'threatening' check on their time-keeping! Long-established staff groups can tend to consider that all is well with the current way of doing things, particularly if the school is considered to be doing a good job. Raising staff awareness in such situations, converting staff who, in accepting the status quo, are passive or actively resistant to change, or who may have competed unsuccessfully for internal appointments, are situations that have been encountered by Rao, Collings and Cutler – the three women headteachers.

Evans, Cutler and Alston all write about teachers who are 'suspicious' of the head or 'management' or of the idea of leadership. Cutler argues that it is important, as a head, to distinguish between issues that are open to negotiation and those subject to consultation only – and to ensure that colleagues know which are which. Research on effective schools has shown how important is the head's judgement of which are the decisions he or she is paid to take responsibility for making, and on which decisions the staff, in order to have ownership, should be able to negotiate.

Not all staff, however, wish for a participatory role in, for example, policy review and formulation, believing, as Collings notes, that it is the head's job to produce policy. For Evans, a major challenge was how to put new ideas into practice yet prove their effectiveness by the traditional yardsticks.

PREJUDICE

Of the female heads, only Collings comments overtly on the sexism she encountered and on how it strengthened her resolve to address equal-opportunities issues in the school. Cutler found it took time for parents to accept 'a youngish woman head' who 'does not quite fit their idea of the charismatic leader'. However, prejudice of another kind – and from several quarters – was encountered by Rao who writes movingly, 'I had to work hard – doubly hard to prove I was a good head, a good, black, headteacher, a good, black, female headteacher. I felt I was in a glass cage . . . I felt very lonely'. It is not, perhaps, surprising that prejudice has been reported. The traditional image of a white, middle-class headmaster is still widely held, despite the increasing number of highly effective headteachers who are women or who are members of black and ethnic minorities. Research carried out some years ago in a large LEA showed that the chances of successful promotion for women were greater than for their male counterparts but, because so many more men applied for promotion, at the end of the day, more males than females were promoted. Clearly the expectations of our society with regard to domestic responsibilities and child care are different for women than for men, but it is important that women who have the skills of leadership are encouraged to put themselves forward for promotion. One way of encouraging this is by drawing attention to successful role models. There are far fewer headteachers from black or ethnic minorities than there are women heads. In this collection of eight chapters two have contributed, but this is a much higher proportion than can be found in the nation's secondary schools. Again, for the future, it is to be hoped that more entrants to the profession will come from minority groups so that appropriate role models will be more common and, in turn, that the number applying and competing successfully for headship will increase. The DES has begun to monitor the ethnicity of student teachers and the 1991 census included some questions relevant to this task. It is to be hoped that the combination of better information on monitoring and more positive action by governing bodies will see a marked reduction in the frequency of prejudice such as that reported here.

STAFF AND PUPIL TURNOVER

In schools located in disadvantaged areas of the inner city, headteachers frequently face a higher-than-average turnover of staff as the suburbs exert the lure of a pleasant home environment and affordable housing in which to raise their own families. For Cutler, however, such difficulties are compounded by an unusually high pupil turnover, allied to a gender imbalance in an area able to provide places in the single-sex schools so often sought by Asian (particularly Muslim) parents. The needs are endless: additional support staff to deal with the almost daily admission and re-admission of students; staff and materials to meet the language needs of the 80 per cent of pupils for whom English is not their first language; and counselling to cope with the culture shock experienced by such diverse pupils as a Kurdish refugee or a student returning from nine months visit to family in rural Bangladesh. In addition to all of this, effort must be made to provide access to a curriculum able to lead to qualifications and equality of opportunity for all. What a challenge for a headteacher.

UNDER-ACHIEVEMENT

Both Flecknoe and Atkinson talk about challenge in relation to under-achievement. For Flecknoe, for example, schools should be places where each student is challenged constantly, and that happens 'wherever they are known best'. Atkinson broadens the discussion, taking it beyond the internal world of the school, to argue that, despite the shortcomings of the system, achievements need to be publicized widely. He believes that there is a need to display a much higher degree of confidence when talking about teachers and schools. The question of national confidence is important. On a recent visit to Singapore we were struck by the level of confidence in, and appreciation of, teachers and schools exhibited by both government and public. The existence of a public holiday dedicated to teachers and annual bonuses related to national output are obvious but telling indicators of this confidence. Just as high expectations appear to work positively for pupils, so they are likely to work positively for teachers and heads.

SCHOOL ORGANIZATION

Reading these chapters, we have been struck by the amount of thought and effort the headteachers put into the organization and management of schools. The size and complexity of the schools and the wide-ranging responsibilities carried out by today's headteachers necessitates a considerable degree of delegation. Different senior management structures have been devised, according to the priorities and preferred management styles of the heads. Most headteachers have three deputies, but Flecknoe favours a slim-line top-management tier, facilitating speedy communications. He has only two deputies (and neither has a clip-board!).

Most of these heads set great store by the development of a team approach. Atkinson believes in the most careful selection of faculty heads and thereafter allows them considerable autonomy. Cutler maintains that delegation helps bond together staff teams. The value of a team approach to whole-school planning and management is stressed by this group of heads. It is also currently in favour among business and commercial organizations as well. The skills required to hold together such teams are considerable – a point not laboured, perhaps because of modesty, by these contributors. Yet an analysis of what he terms 'the micro-politics of schools' by Professor Stephen Ball of King's College, London, reveals the web of conflicting pressures that bear upon the head of a school.

THE ORGANIZATION OF LEARNING

When it comes to the organization and management of learning, Alston considers schools have much to learn from the business world. In his view, a whole-school approach, via a school development plan, is the way to ensure consistent change and improvement. In Leggatt's Ontario school, the development, implementation and evaluation of the school plan have achieved considerable levels of sophistication. In Britain, the formal use of school development plans, however, is relatively new.

Time will tell whether they prove useful to heads in such situations. They certainly have the potential to do so requiring, as they do, a realistic appraisal of the strengths and weaknesses of the school, a plan to build on the strengths and correct these identified weaknesses and the regular monitoring and evaluation of the success of changes. Changing schools, for the better, however, is difficult. Michael Fullan, the Professor of Education at the University of Toronto, an expert involved in school change, believes it takes up to between five and seven years to 'turn a school around'. Perhaps in our fast-moving modern world this time can be shortened: hence Alston's comments about the business world where the decision time is often shorter.

PARENTAL AND COMMUNITY INVOLVEMENT

Attempts to involve parents in the life of the school and the education of their sons and daughters raises many issues for these headteachers. Parents from minority-ethnic groups, lacking fluency in English or ill-informed about the British education system, may be loath to visit the school. Many parents at both Cutler's and Rao's schools, fearful of racial harassment, are unwilling to leave their homes after dark in order to attend meetings. At the extreme, some of the most disadvantaged families living in cities do not have homes to call their own. In London, in particular, there are

considerable numbers of families living in bed-and-breakfast accommodation. The impact of this on their children's education is likely to be
devastating. It would require the most dedicated student to be able to
concentrate at a time of such family uncertainty and emotional upheaval.

It is clear from these accounts that parents' different value systems and
attitudes towards education can create barriers towards schools and
teachers and can result in suspicion (of them). Thus Rao had to work hard
to encourage some of her Muslim parents to ease some of the restrictions
imposed on their daughters. Flecknoe, on the other hand, comments on the
traditional respect for the teaching profession held by many from the
Indian sub-continent. He quotes a parent-governor: 'My father took me to
school and said to me – "this teacher is now also your father" – and he said
to the teacher – "here is your son!" '

Where a degree of parental involvement is achieved, it is (in Atkinson's
view) far too precious to be wasted on fund-raising. In his view, the thrust
of such activity should be to inform parents and to deepen their understanding of the work of the school. This is a view similar to Collings, who
sees parents as 'education consultants' and uses them as a sounding-board
on 'the changes in school policy that will affect them'.

Evans faces a somewhat different challenge: how to foster school–
community links in a school whose constituency is city-wide. Setting up the
Trinity Association, with a membership of parents of current and former
pupils, staff, governors and other friends of the school, was one way of
meeting this challenge. Alston writes that open enrolment, under which
parents may choose to send their child to any school of their choice, has
made headteachers even more conscious of the need to be aware of and
react to parents' concerns lest the bush telegraph at the school gates under-
mines the best-laid marketing plans. Atkinson holds individual daytime appointments with prospective pupils and their parents prior to secondary
enrolment in order to build up a personal relationship with them before the
start of the school year. Staff at Collings' school are briefed to be welcoming
and sensitive to parents' requests and the induction course for new staff
includes the issue of listening to parents. At a time of the consumer power of
parents in education, these approaches appear wise. The days when schools
could be casual, if not contemptuous, of parental feelings are long since gone.

PERSONAL REFLECTIONS

In concluding their personal reflections at least two contributors complain
that the job allows little time for reflection. Time pressures and time

management are noted by most contributors – usually in terms of insufficiency or inadequacy. Two headteachers, however, refer to the risks inherent in being a headteacher of a particular school for too great a period of time. Thus, Alston quotes Wilde's epigram that 'after seven years we begin to destroy what we have created' and Flecknoe comments that 'schools actually benefit from the nervous energy of the insecurity of a head's first few years and suffer from the contentment induced by comfort!' Alston sees a solution in short-term contracts; Flecknoe is thinking of buying a hair shirt! Interestingly, research carried out in primary schools shows that seven years is indeed a good time for a head's duration. It was found that the first three years were needed for the head to establish him or herself, the good years were between three and seven but this was followed by a period in which the risk of growing stale increased.

Most headteachers express an appreciation of their power to get things done, to be an enabler of change and to be able to deploy resources in the pursuit of effective education. Evans, however, considers he had more direct power as a head of department; what he considers he has now is influence. In a slightly different vein, Atkinson reiterates his belief in the power of the school to affect pupils' life chances. Again, research backs up this argument and shows that, while attainment at any age is likely to be influenced strongly by family background, *progress* within school is more susceptible to the influence of the school itself.

While acknowledging the exhilaration, the risks, the responsibilities and the rewards in making change happen in shaping a school, the pace of externally enforced, recent changes leads some of these headteachers to plea for respite and for stability. Leggatt, however, acknowledges the encouragement and resources for the innovation he has received. On the UK side of the Atlantic, headteachers face a different situation. Alston comments on 'the dual problems of low pay and low public esteem' and Collings argues that 'bureaucratic inflexibility and a deskilled teaching force are hardly a recipe for success'.

The problems concerned with the low morale of teachers are serious. They stem from a variety of factors. One factor is pay, which, since the mid-1970s, has declined in relation to a number of comparable occupations. Another, and one that is related, is the negative impact of the industrial action carried out during the 1980s as a reaction to the declining levels of pay. The third fact, also related to the first two, is the action of the then Secretary of State in suspending the pay-negotiating machinery and assuming the powers to determine teachers' salaries. A fourth factor is the imposition of a contract and conditions of service on the teaching profession as part of the Education Act 1987. Coupled with all this, not surprisingly, has been an apparent increase in the number of teachers seeking early retirement and a severe shortage of recruits to certain specializations. This is the situation into which the details of the Education Reform Bill were first revealed. The subsequent developments with regard to the implementation of the Act have been well described by these eight heads.

In considering the converse of all this gloom (the rewards of headship) the group presents a range, from the everyday to the more grandiose, from the immediate to the potential. For Collings, reward lies in a pupil's cheery wave and smile; for Alston, it is in the observation of a good lesson well-taught. Becoming the first black, female, headteacher was way beyond the dreams of Rao when she first came to the UK. In Atkinson's eyes, the rewards of being a head lie in the support and trust of parents and the commitment of colleagues. Flecknoe enjoys transformation of his pupils from the powerless to the powerful. Evans writes that 'it is a privilege to be able to influence a school and its community, to have a vision of education and the possibility of realizing it'.

These are worthy sentiments and, in our view, these eight contributors have survived the upheavals and learnt to cope with the new situation. This process has not been easy and scars have been revealed in some of the chapters. The overriding impression that we have gained, however, is positive. These heads have survived the heat, they have developed their skills, they are ready to take their schools into the new order. Yet, as their comments make clear, they have not lost sight of their aims. They deserve support and they need encouragement, as do all the others not represented in these chapters. It is in the hands of these heads and their colleagues that the development of the future generations of our society lie.

Index